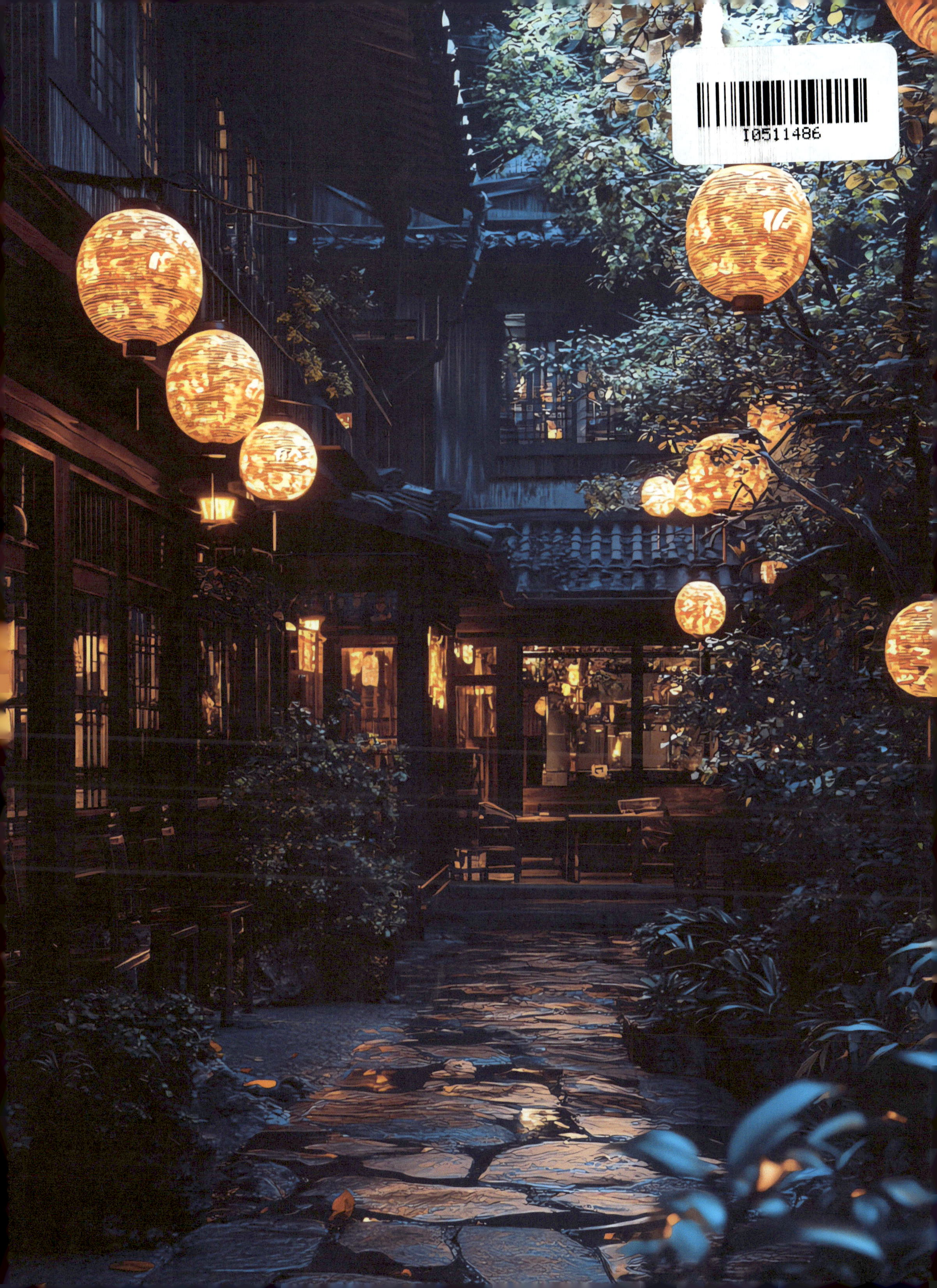

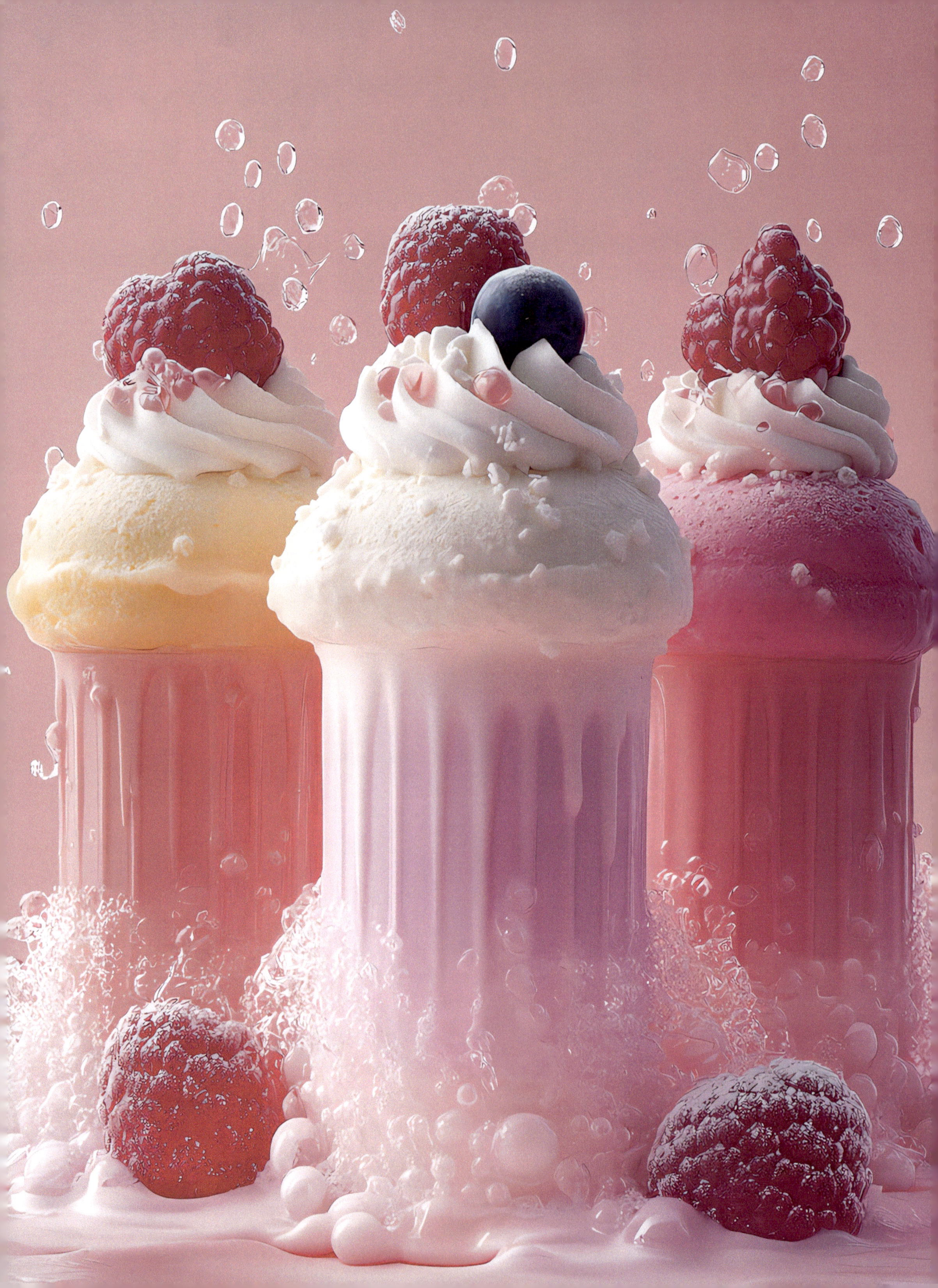

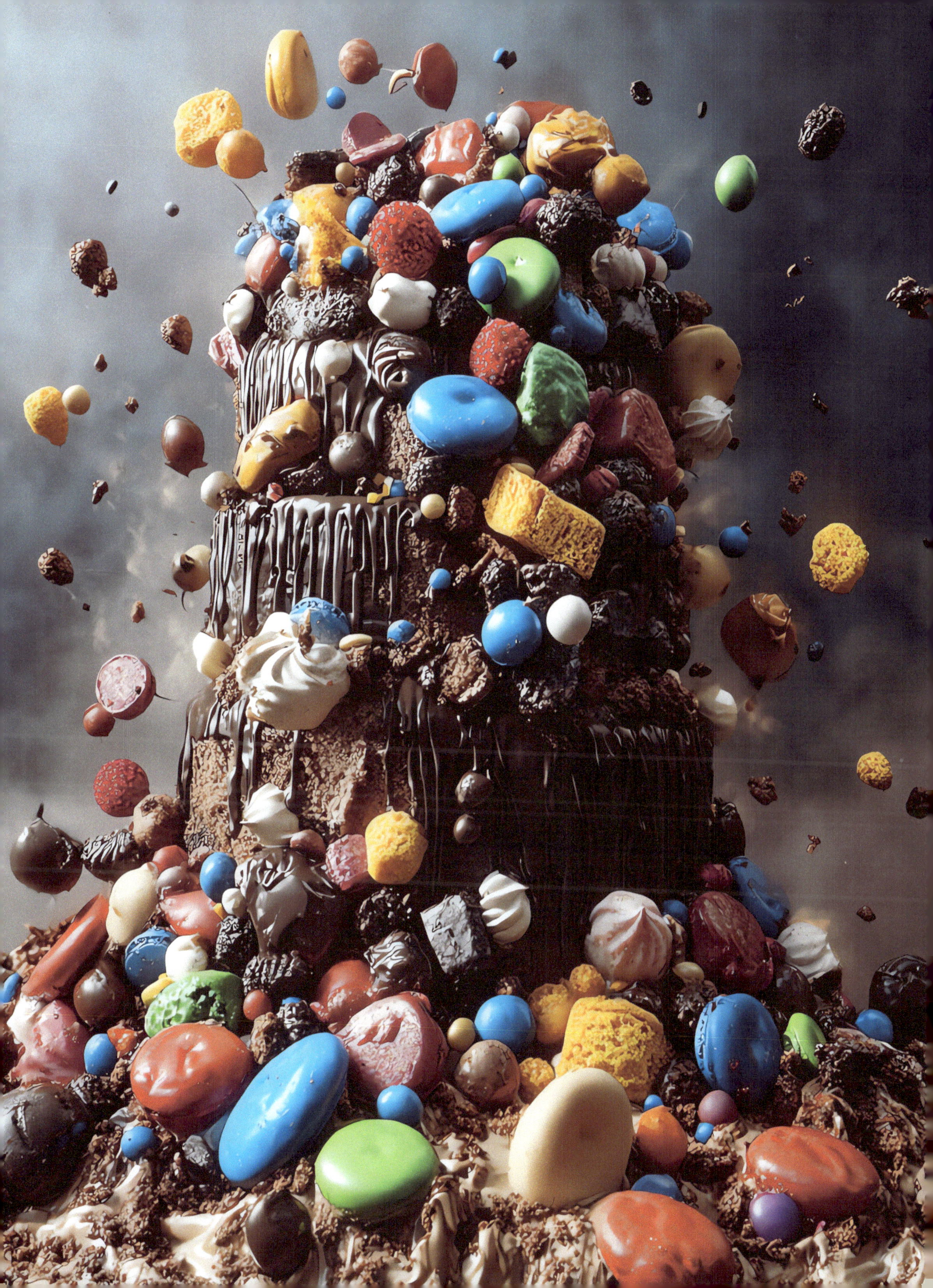

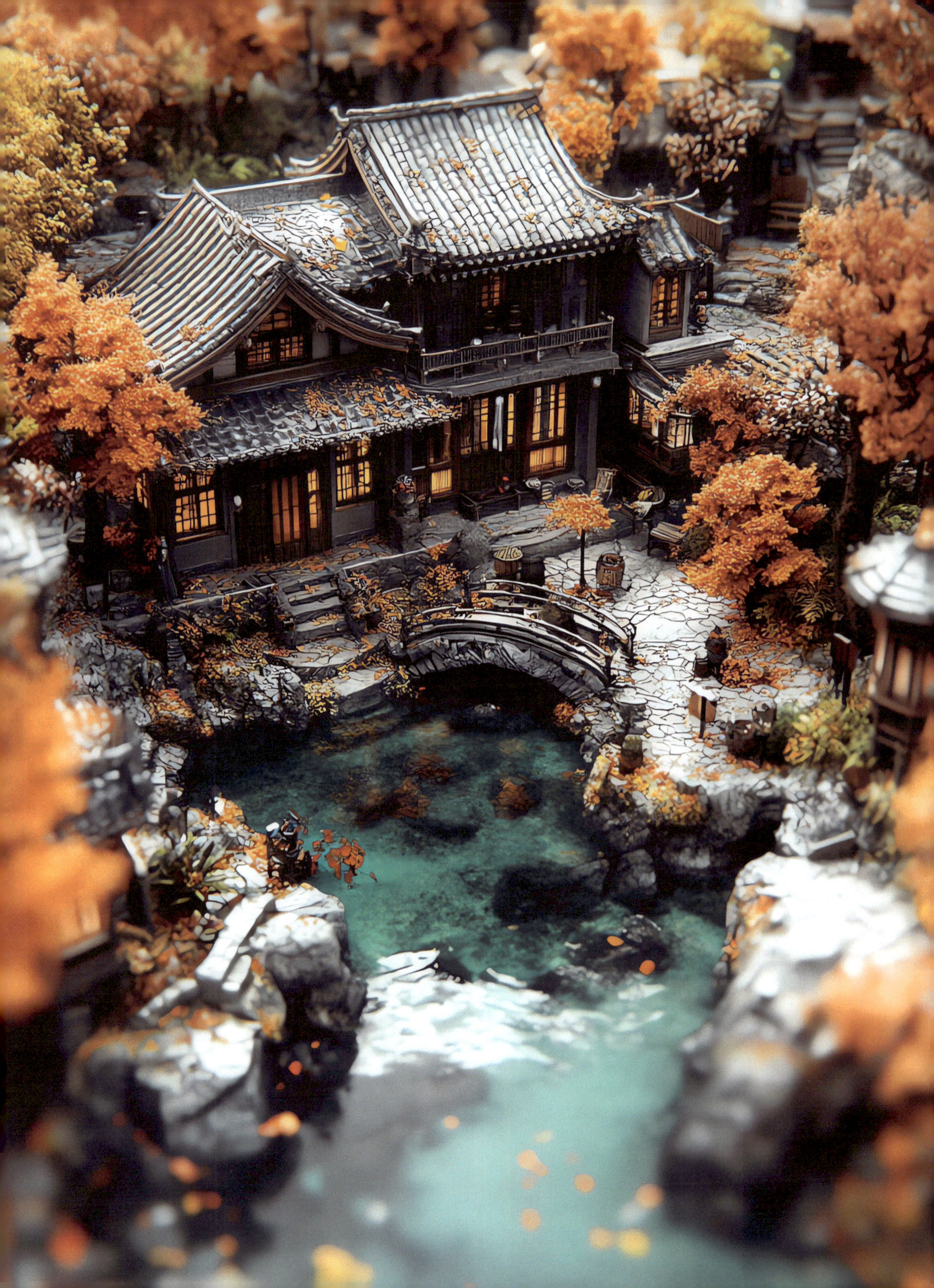

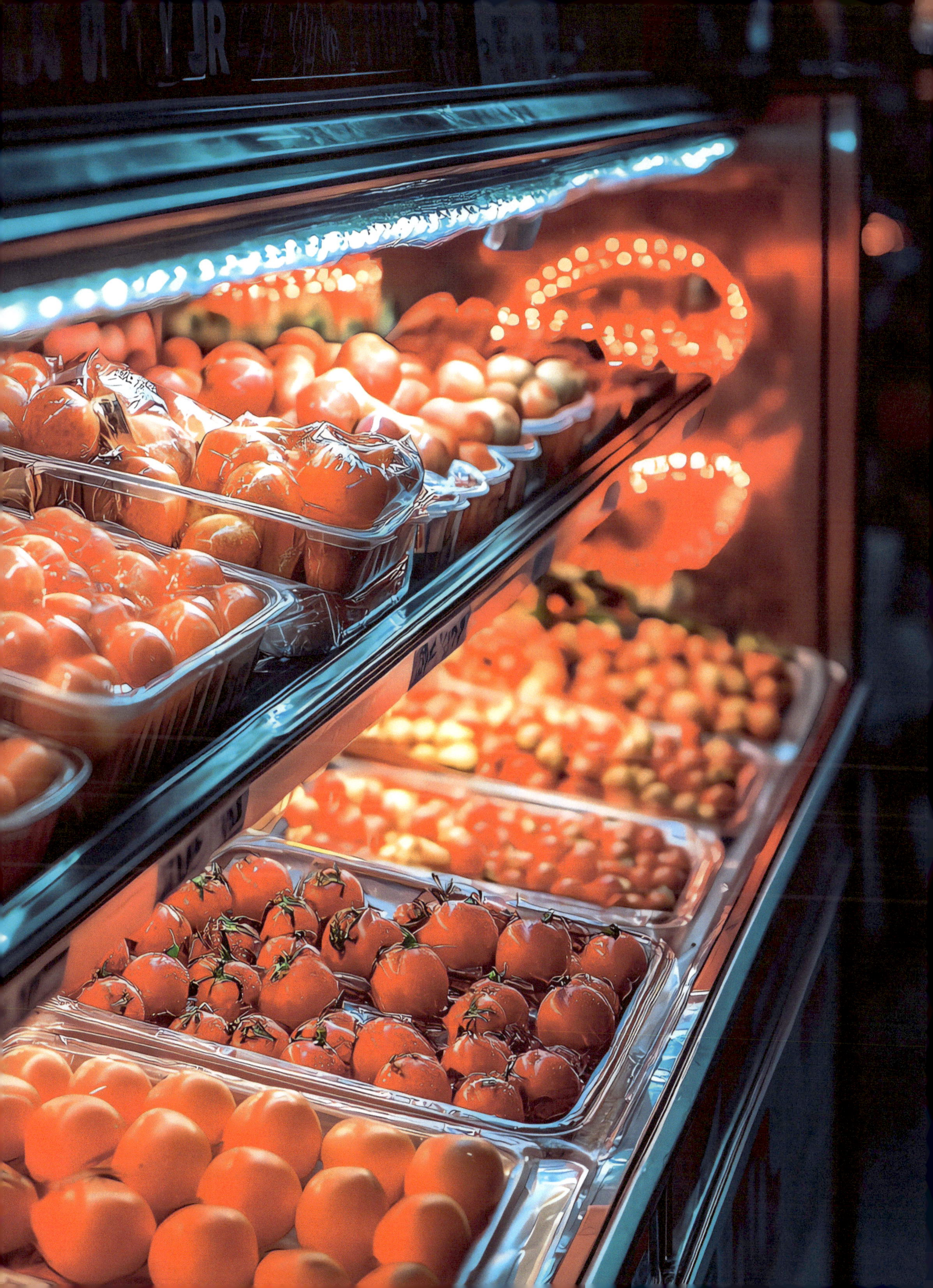

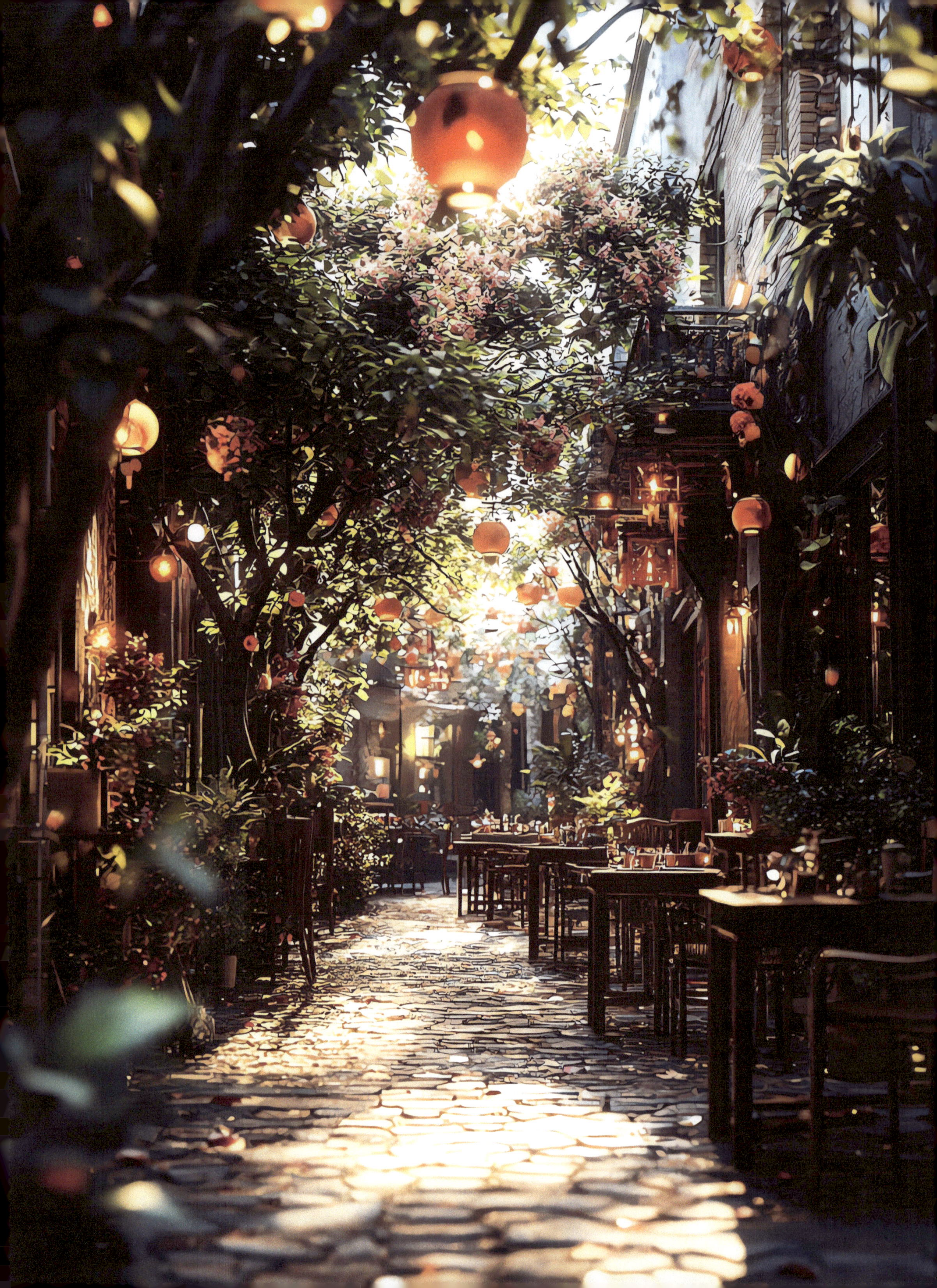

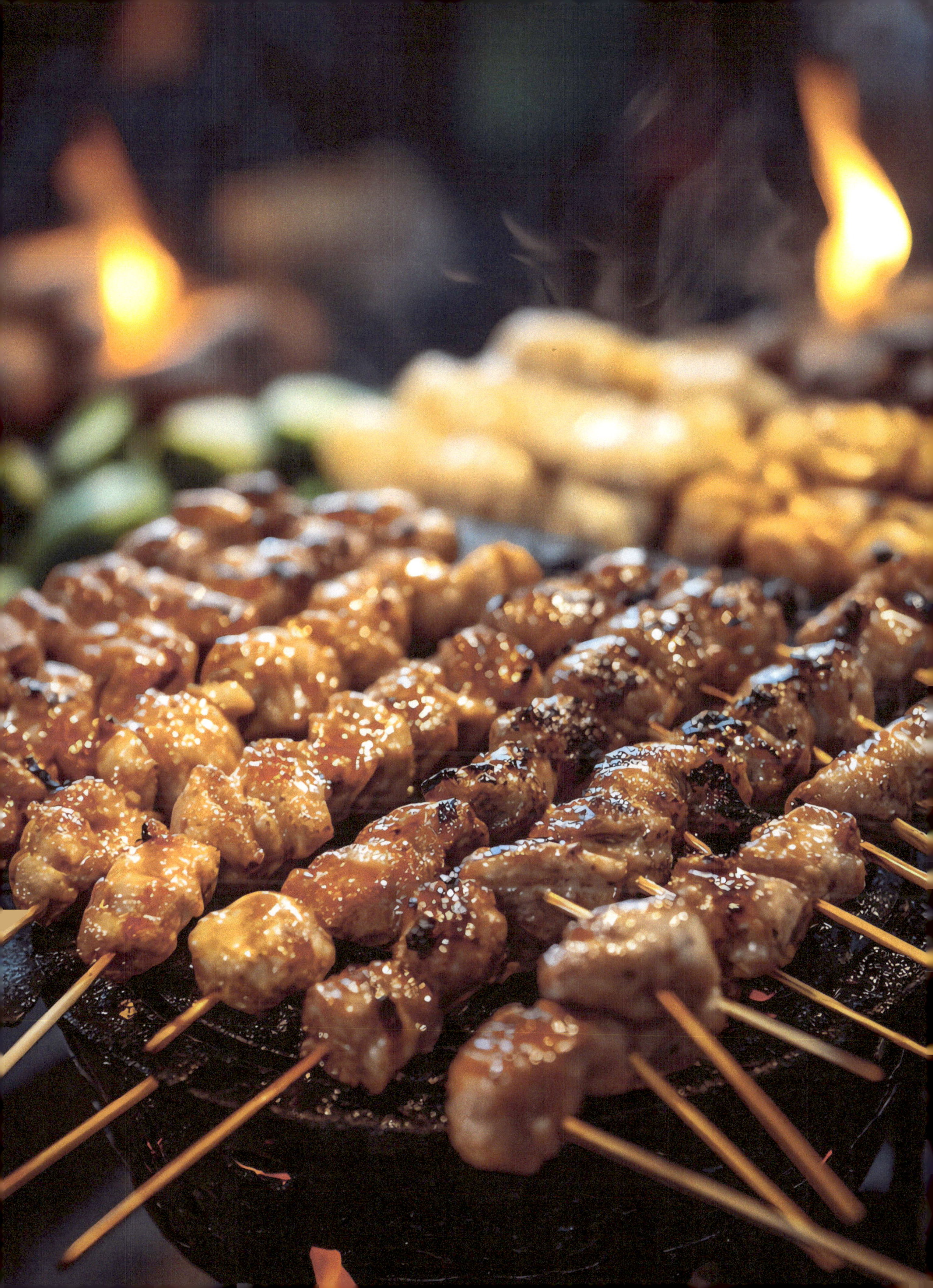

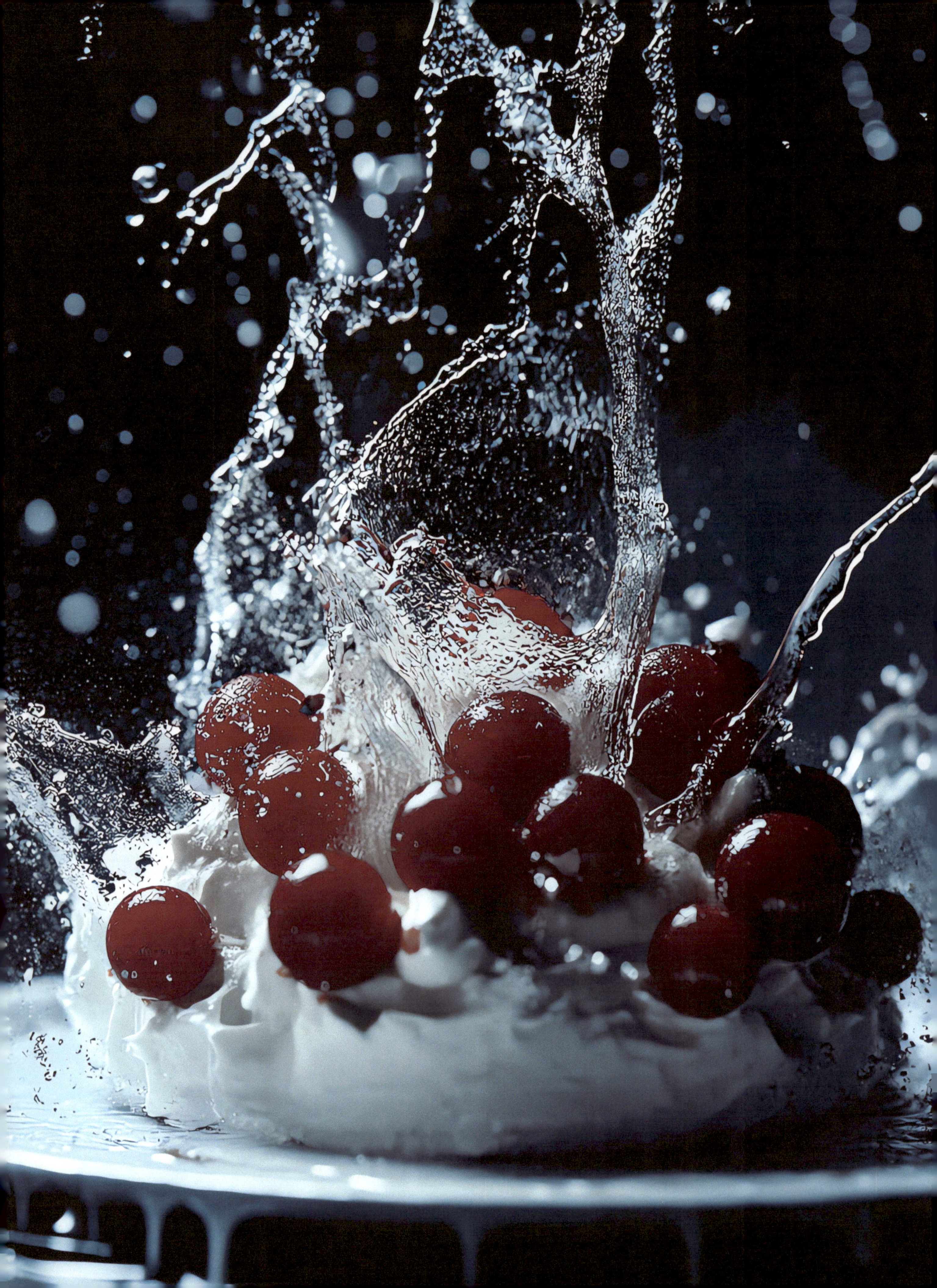

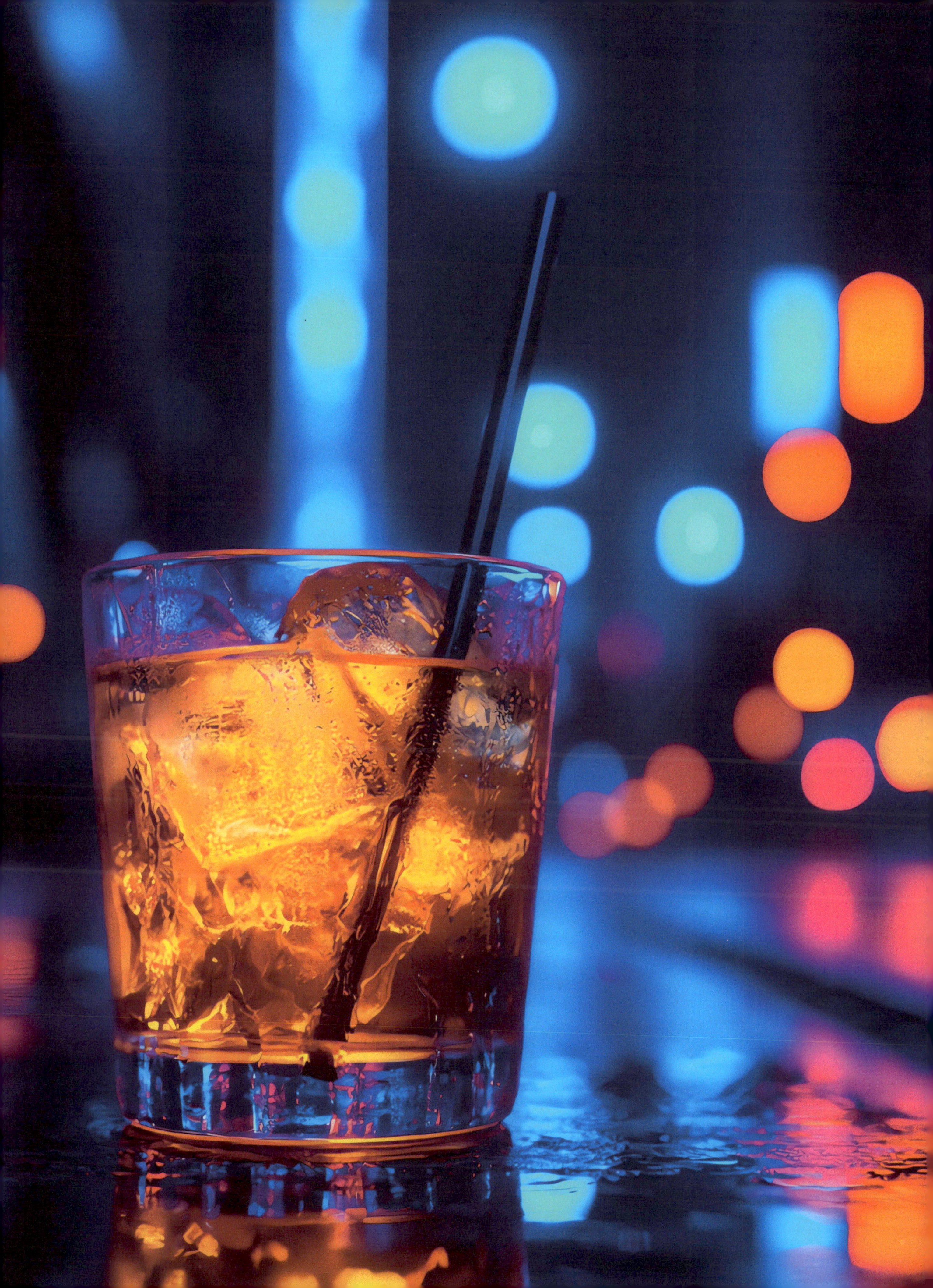

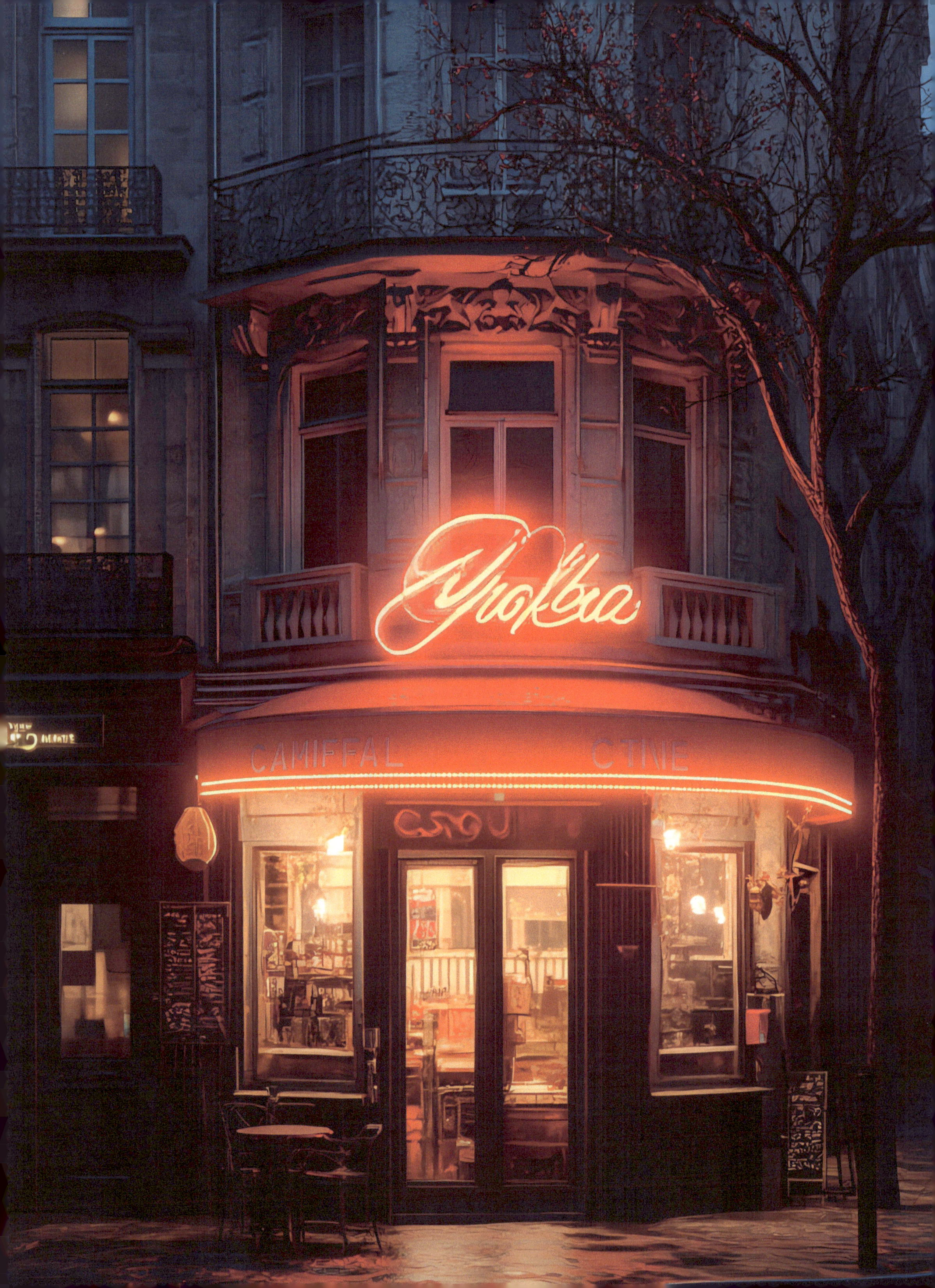
CAMIFFAL
CTINE

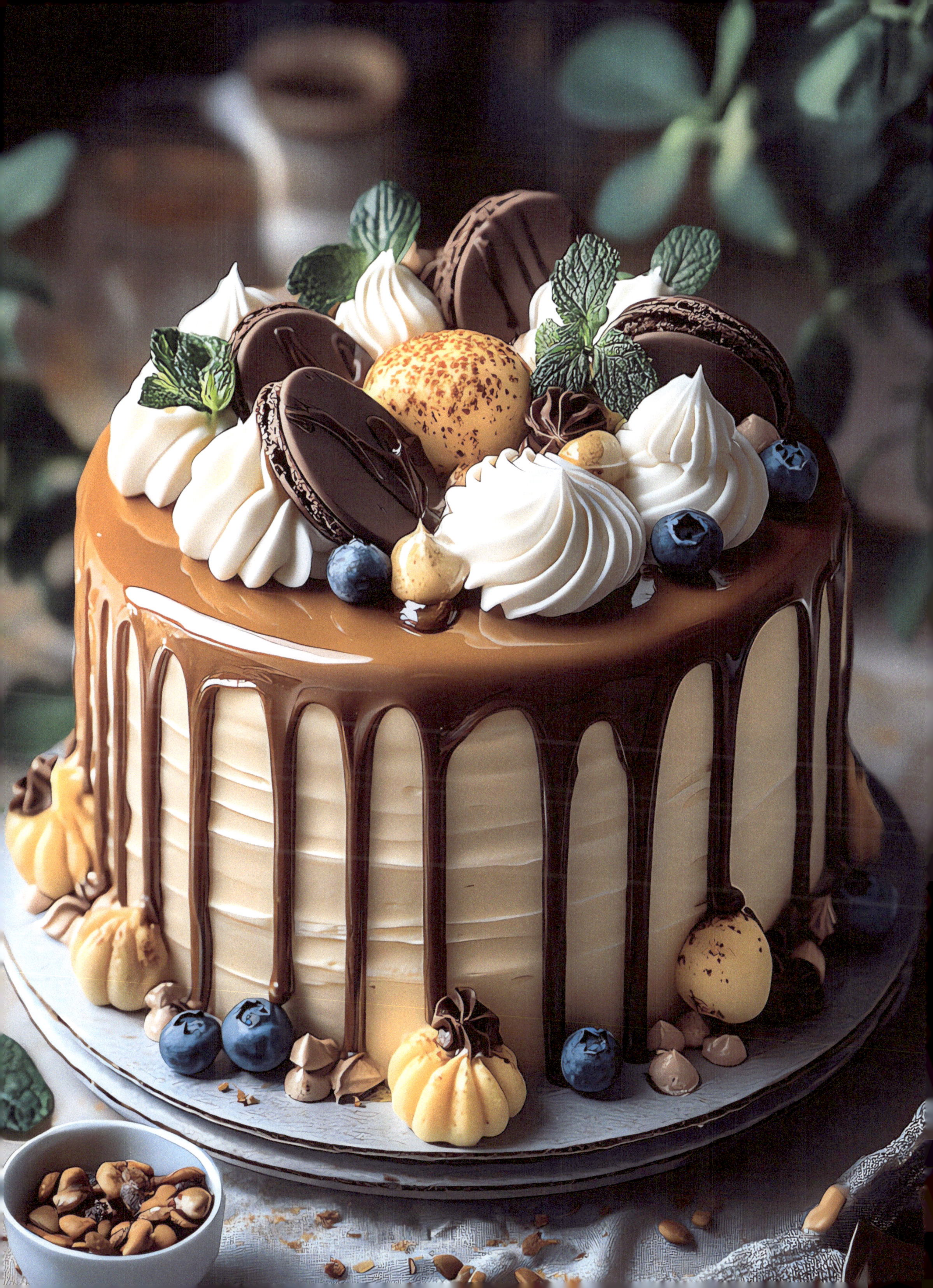

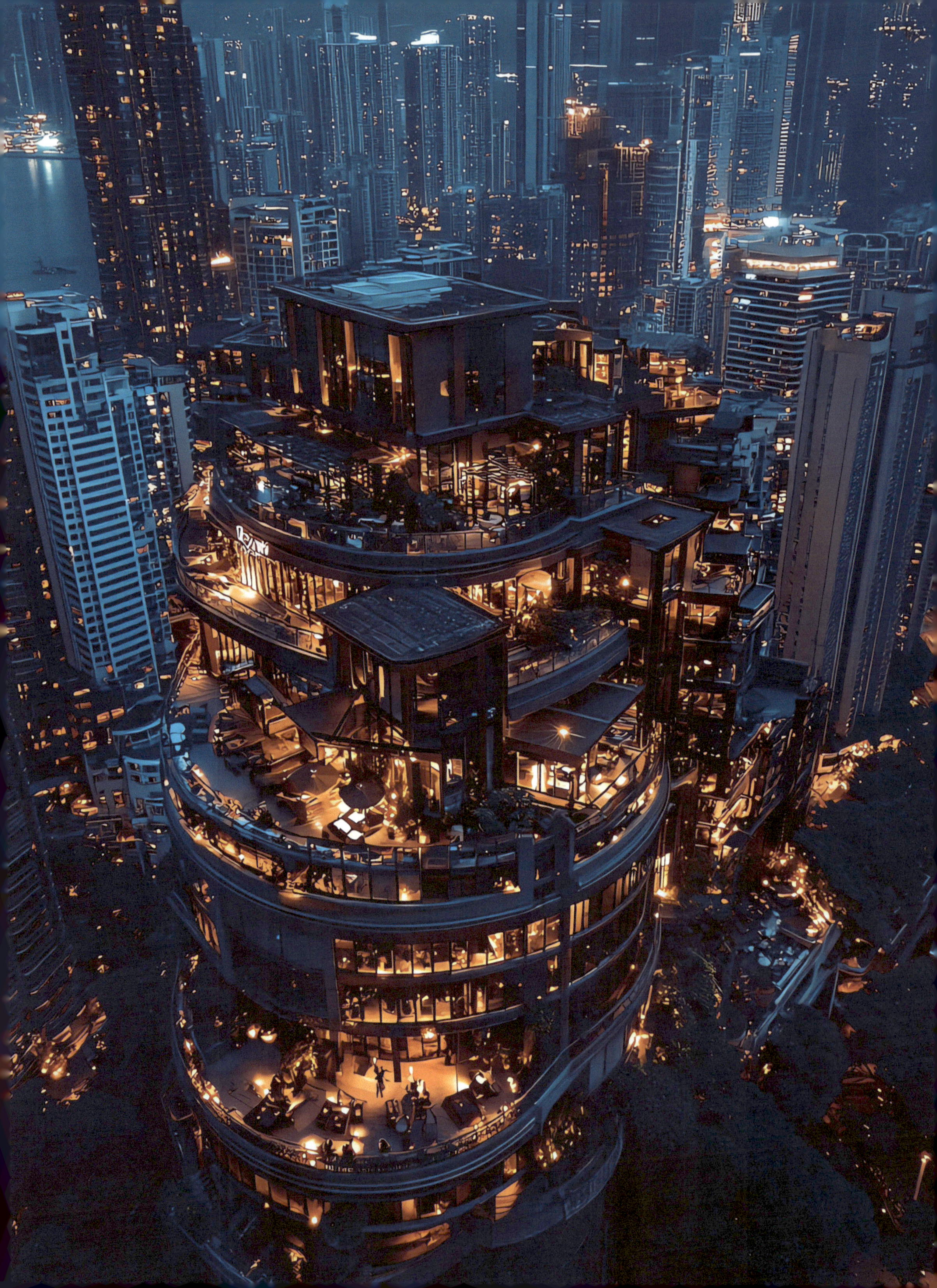

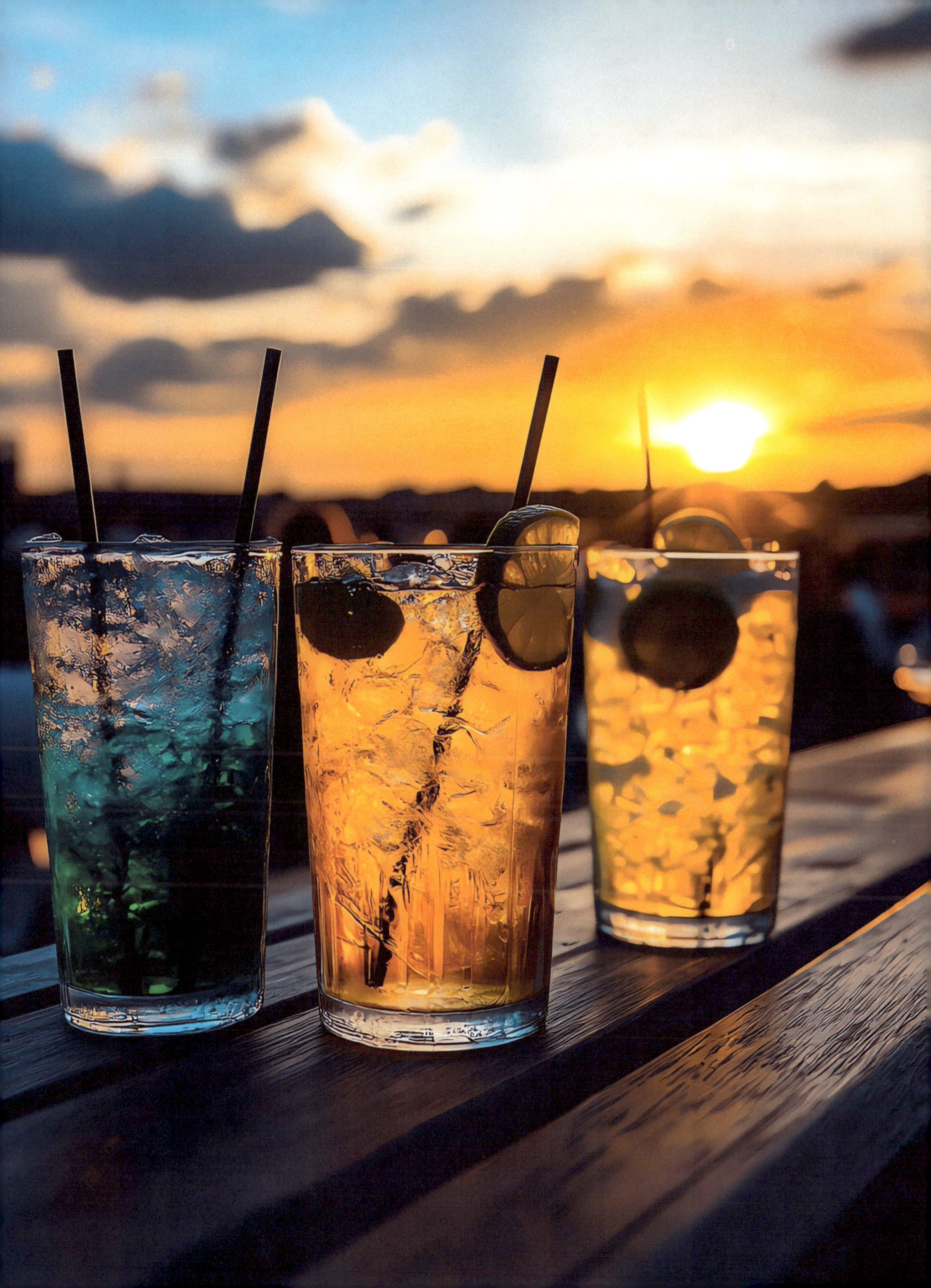

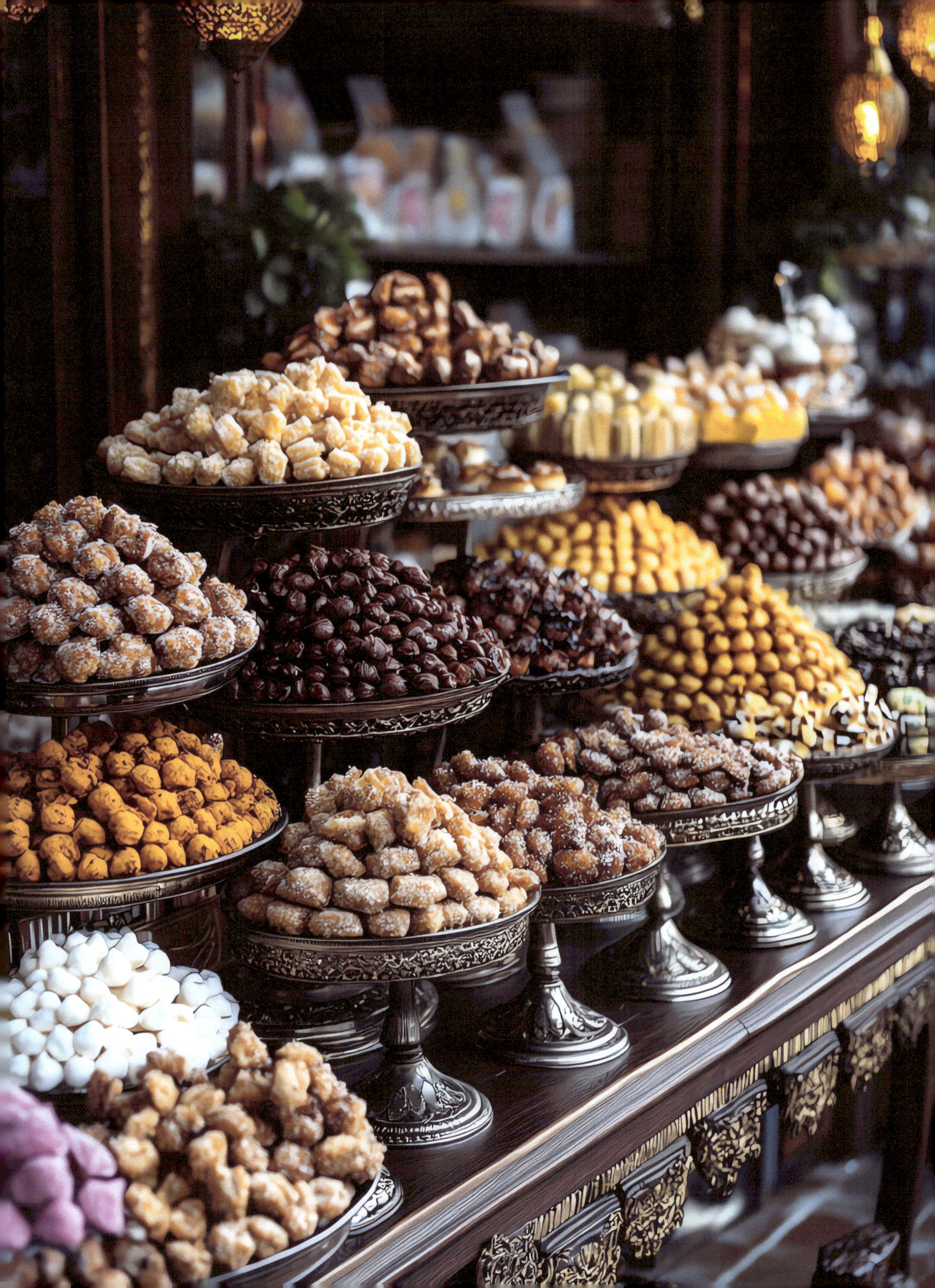

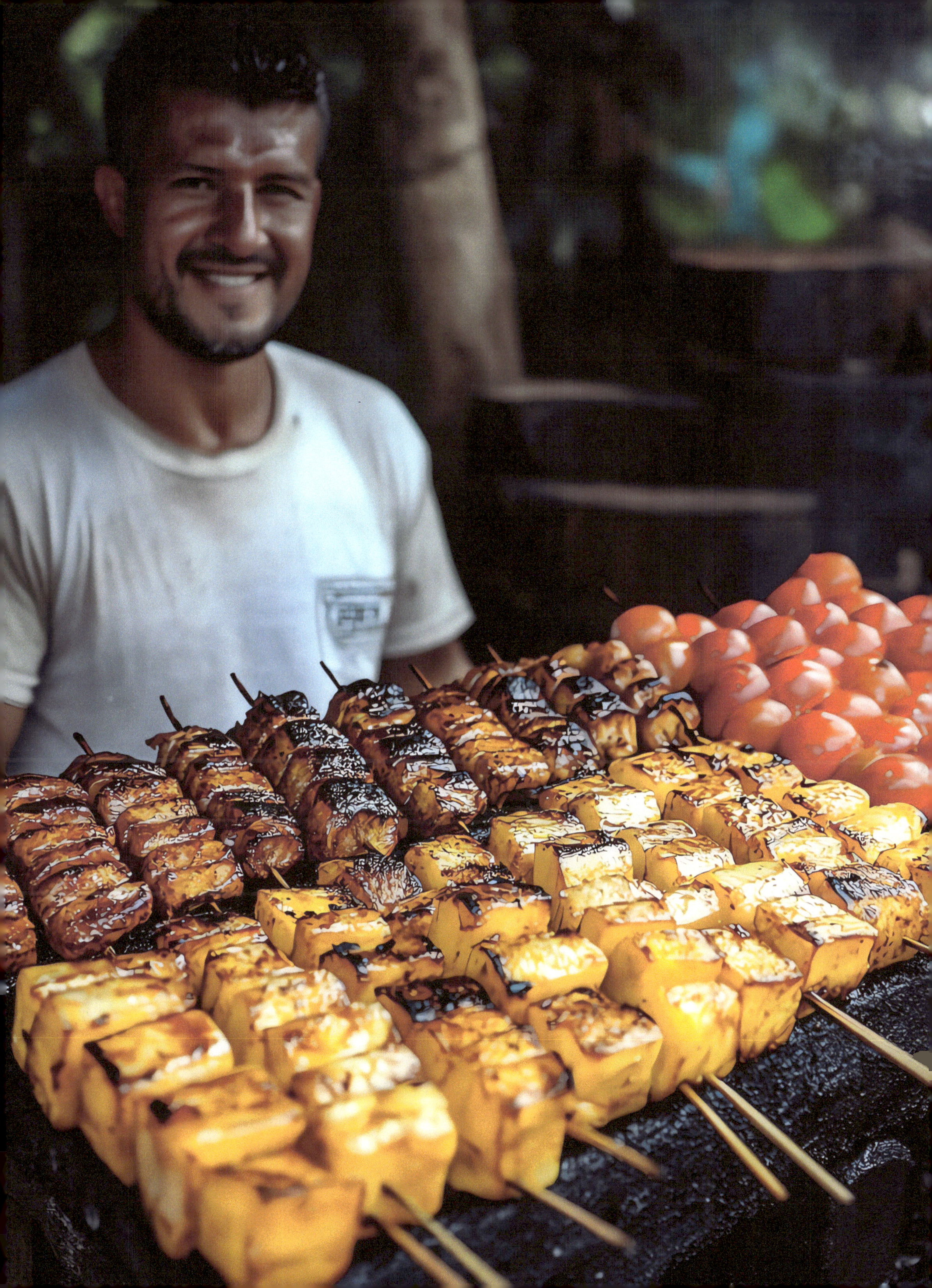

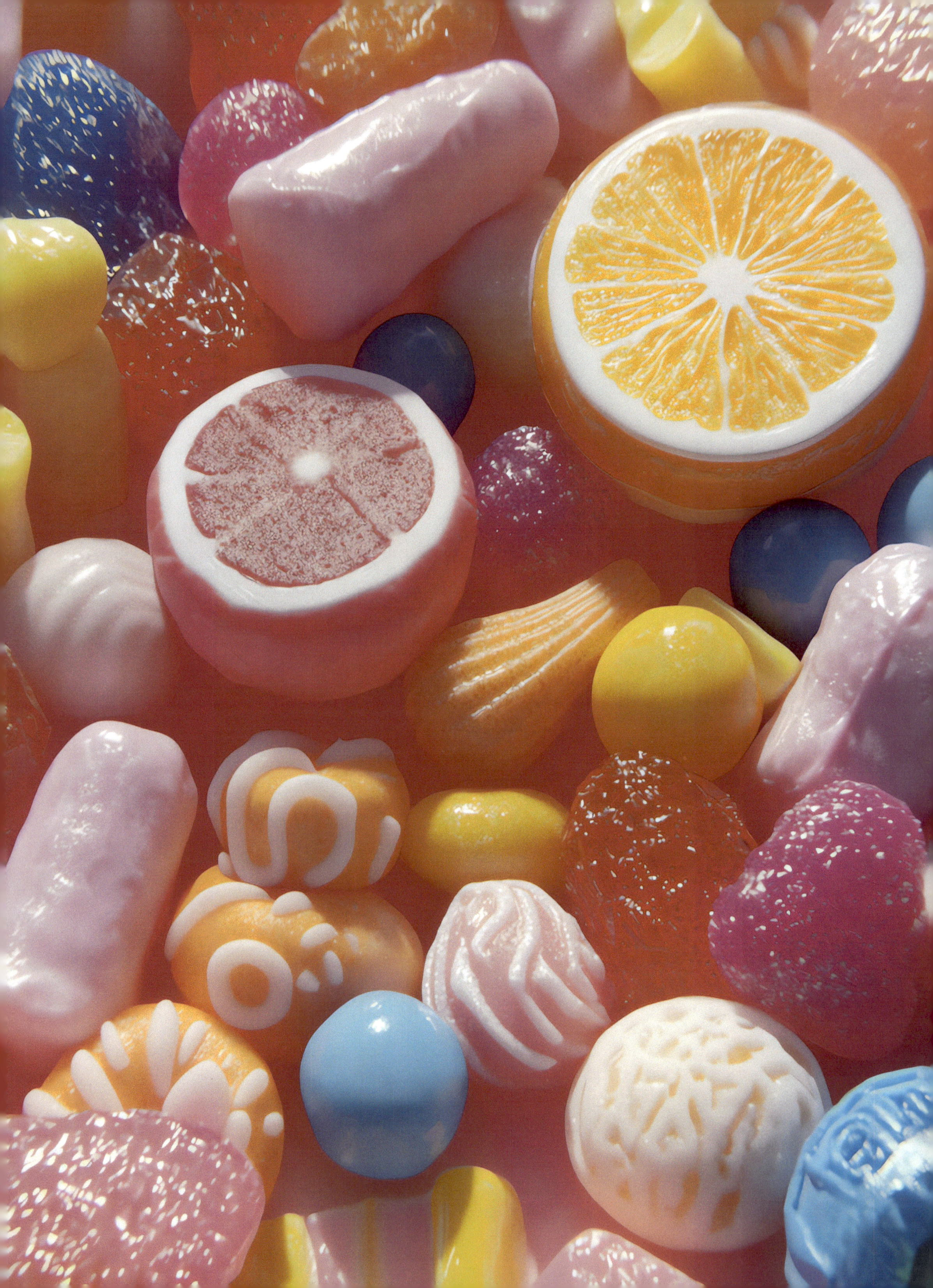

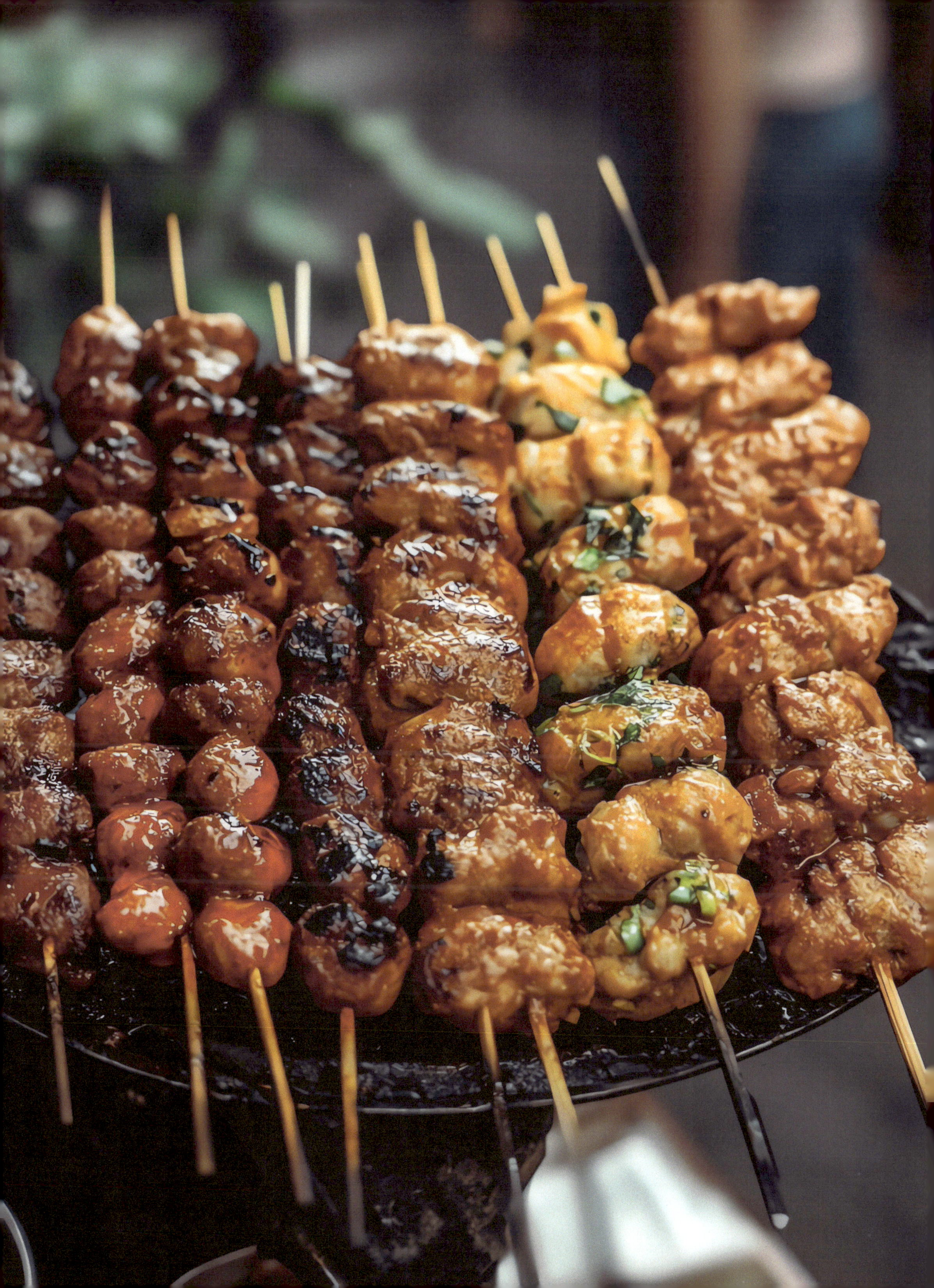

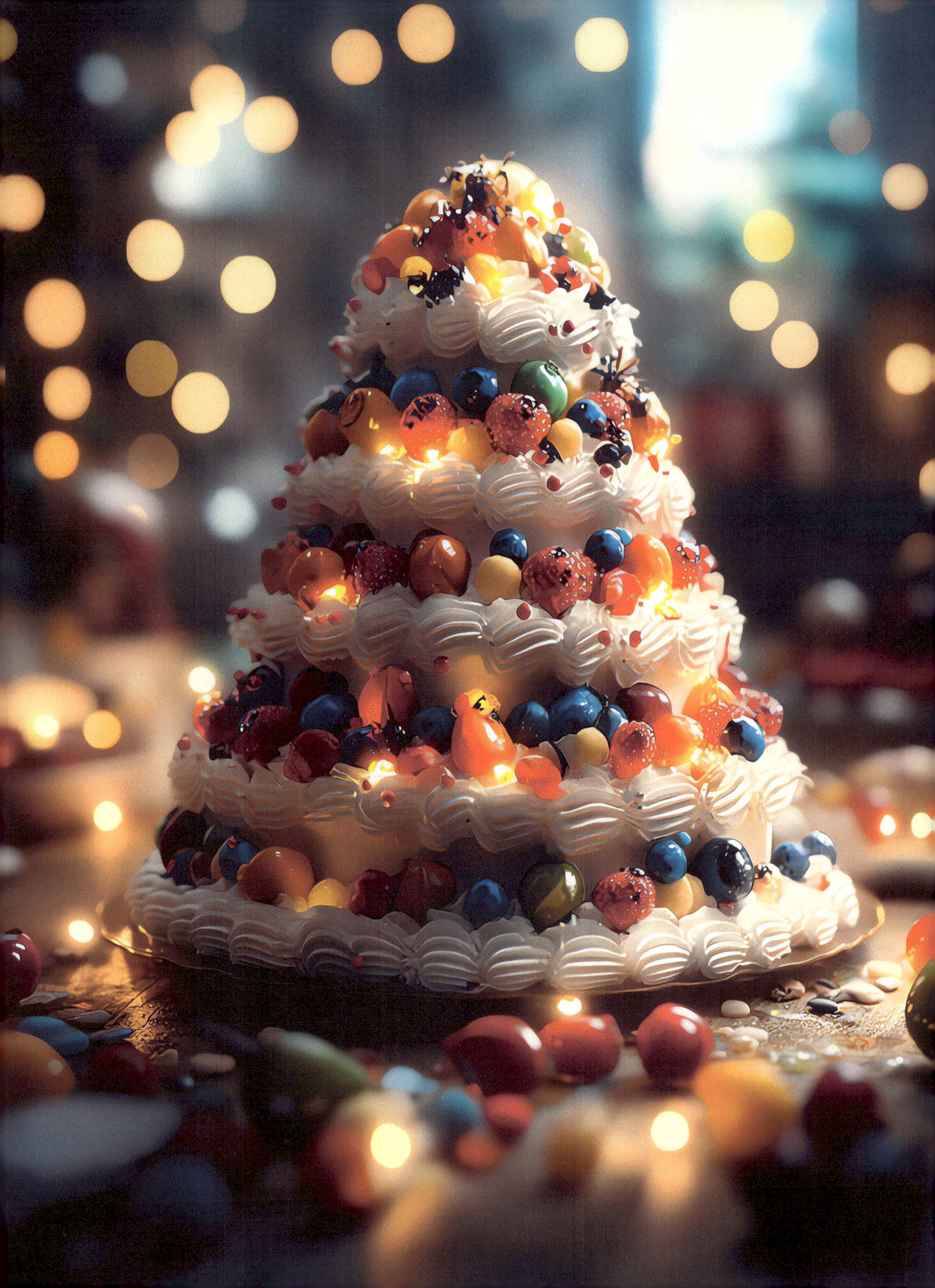

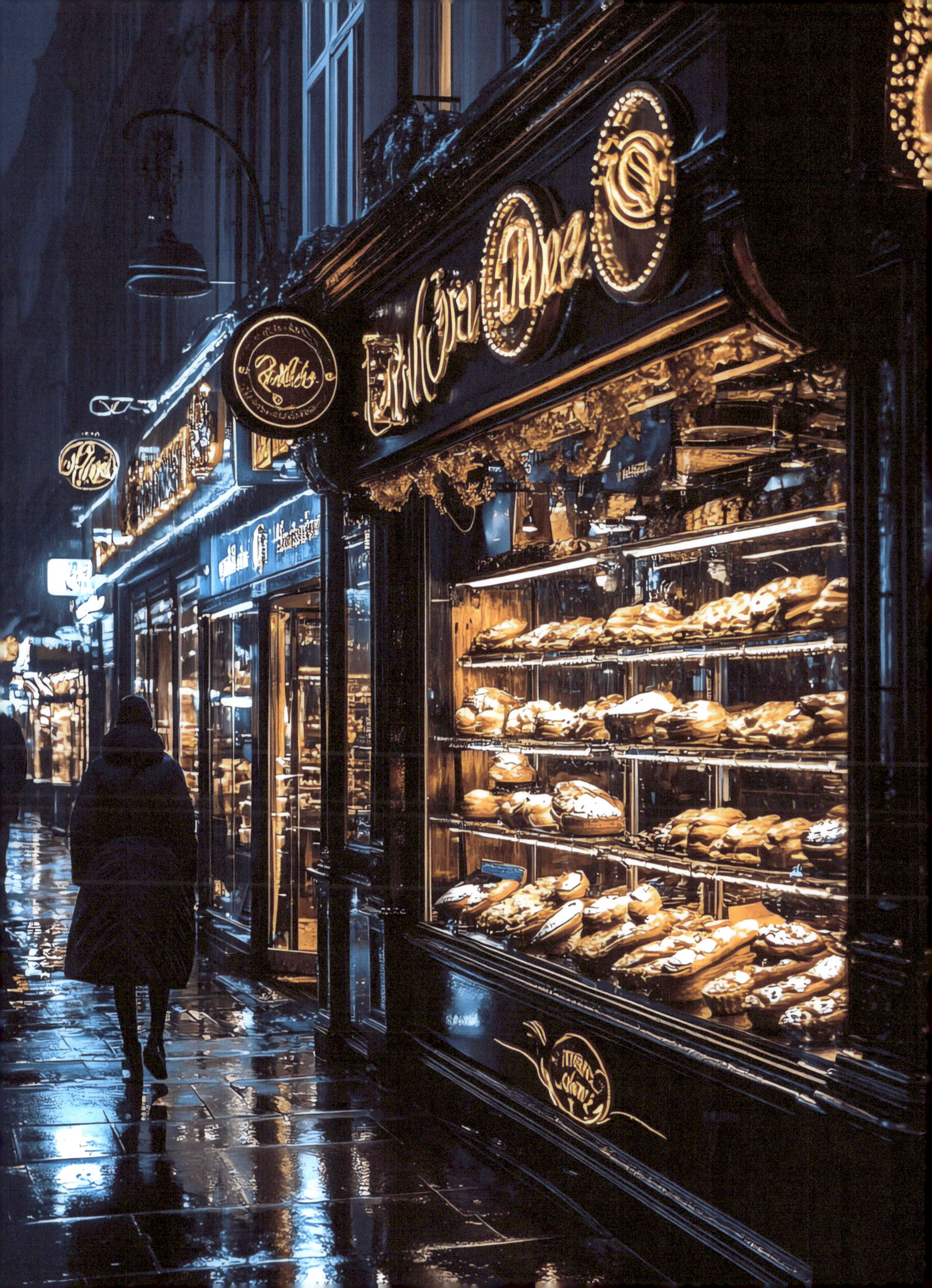

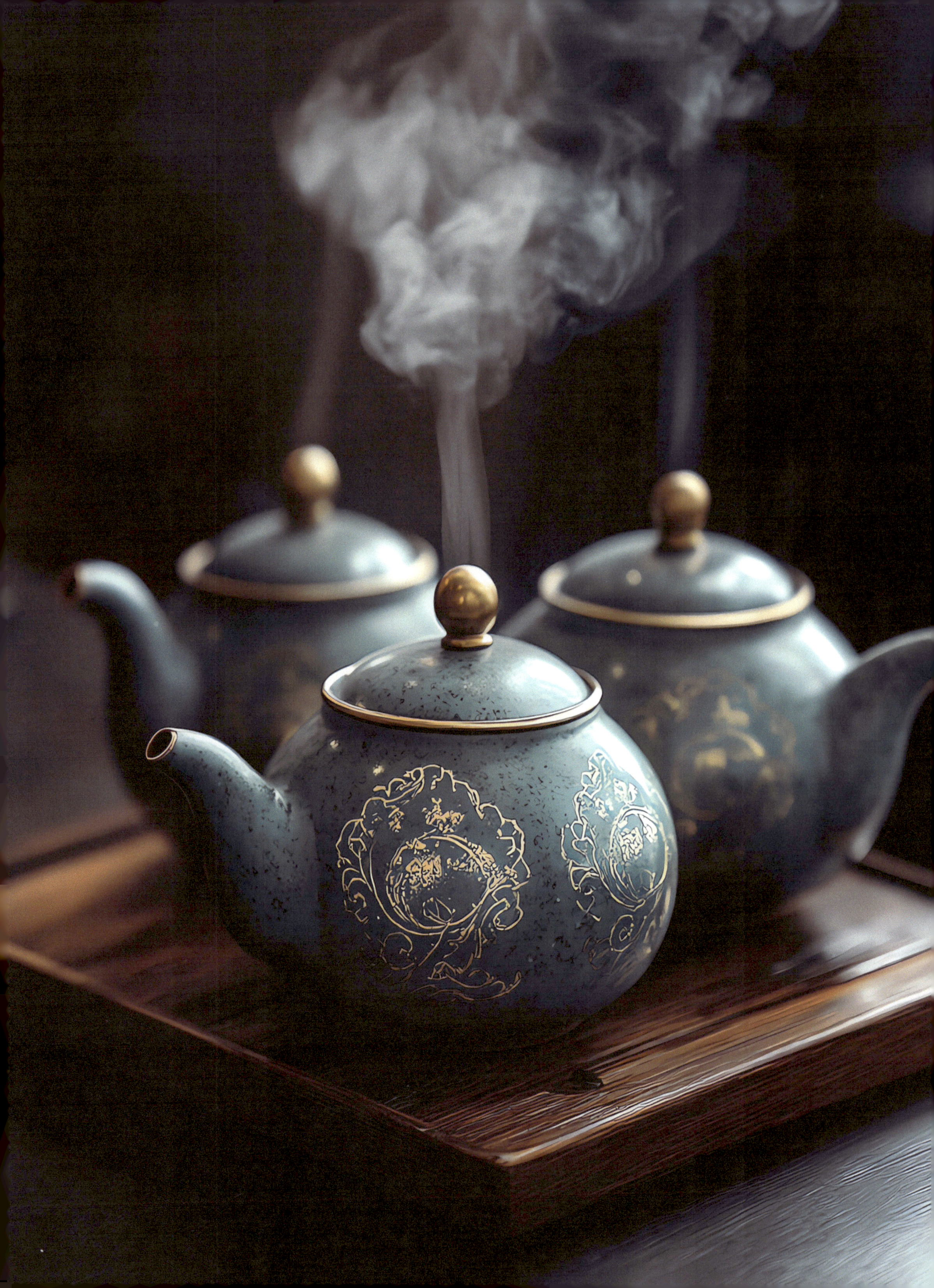

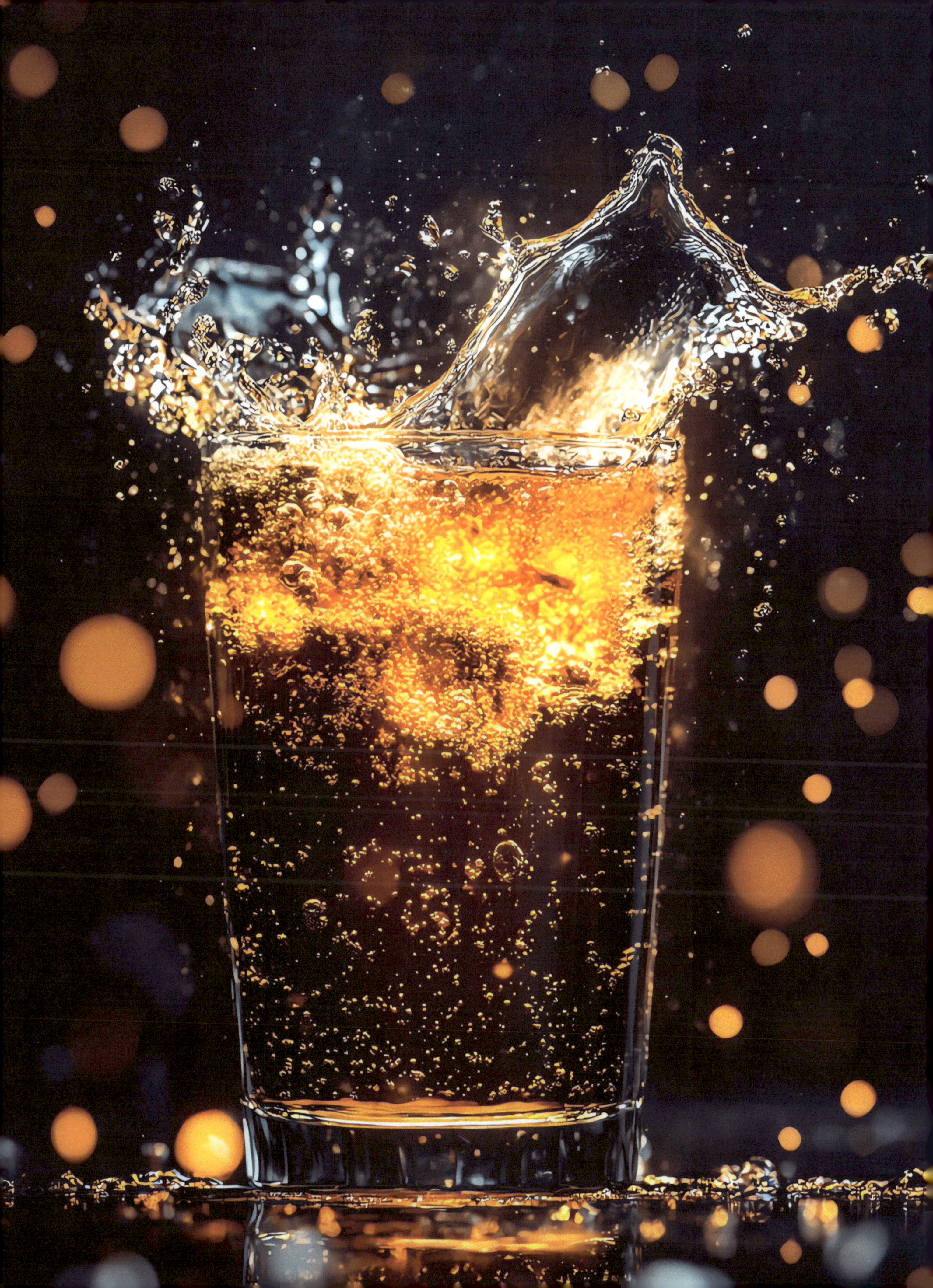

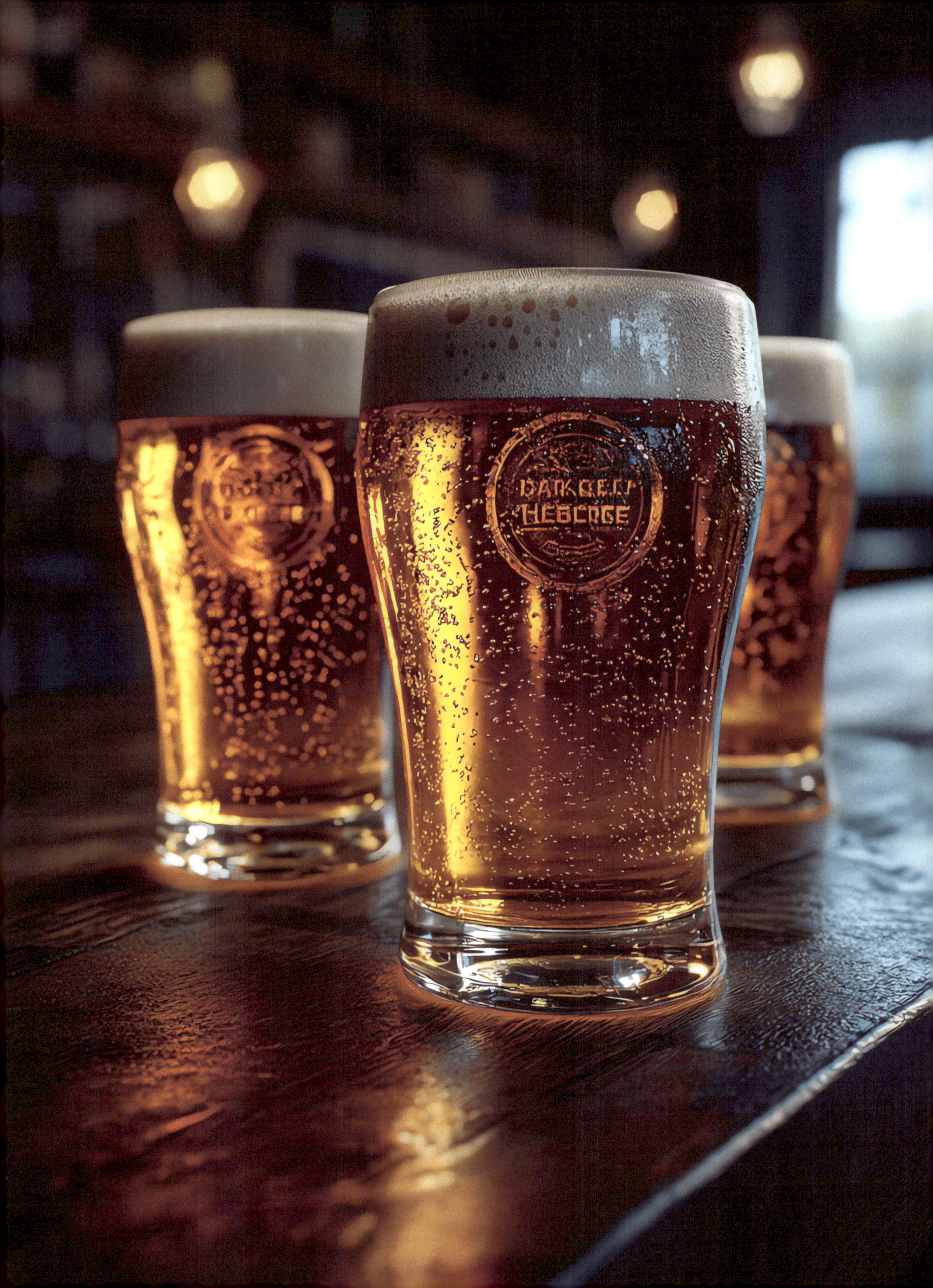

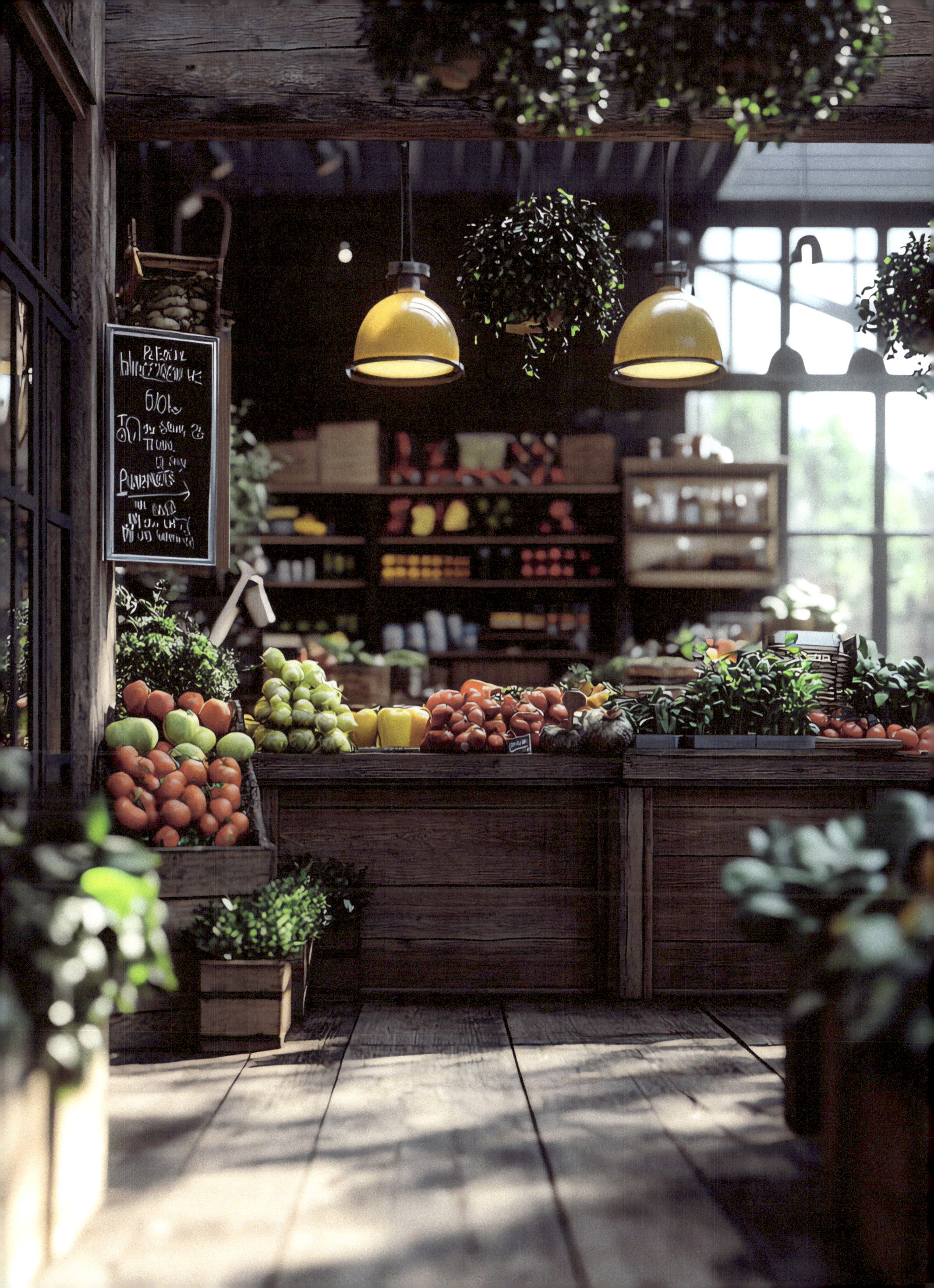

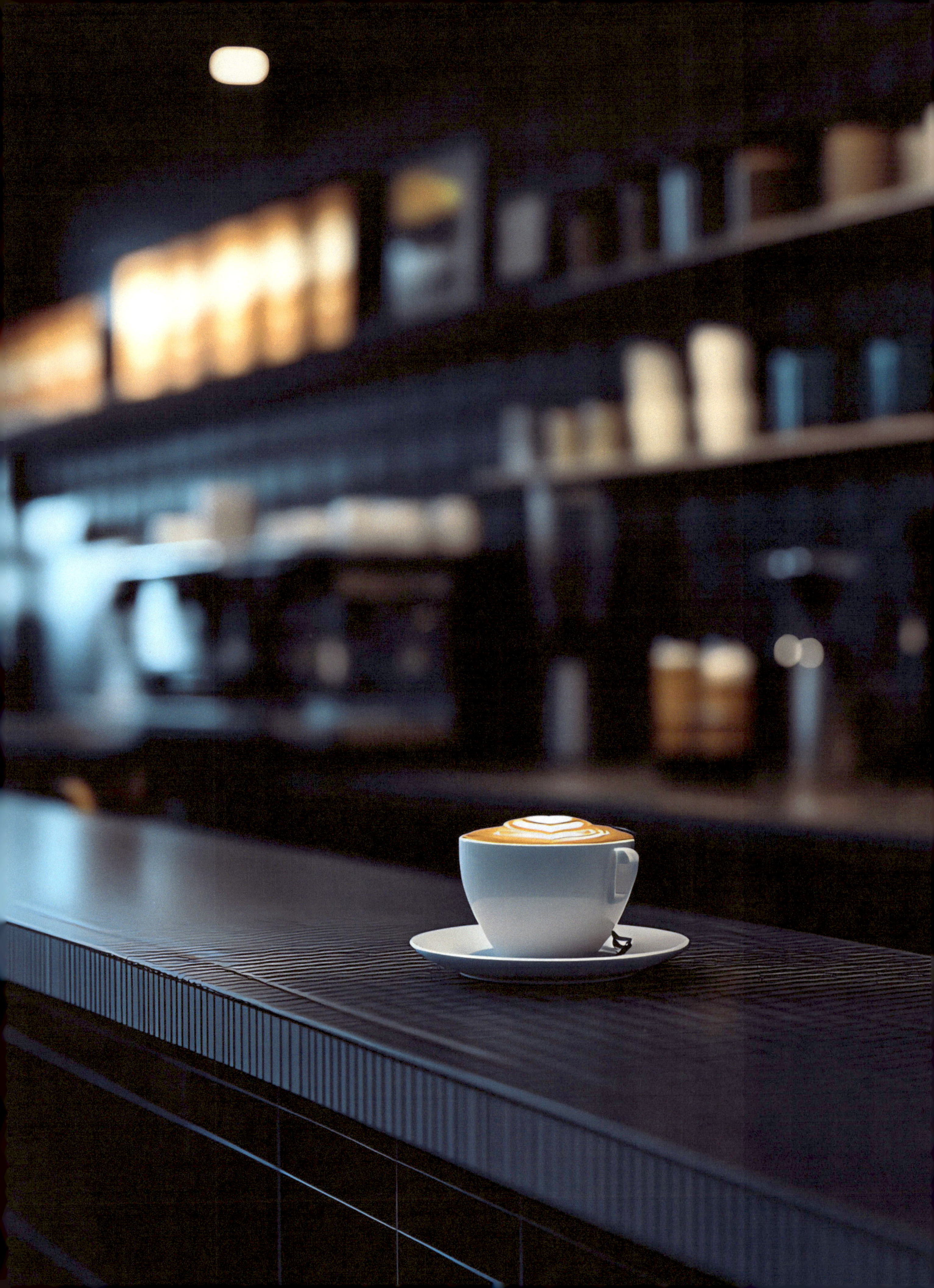

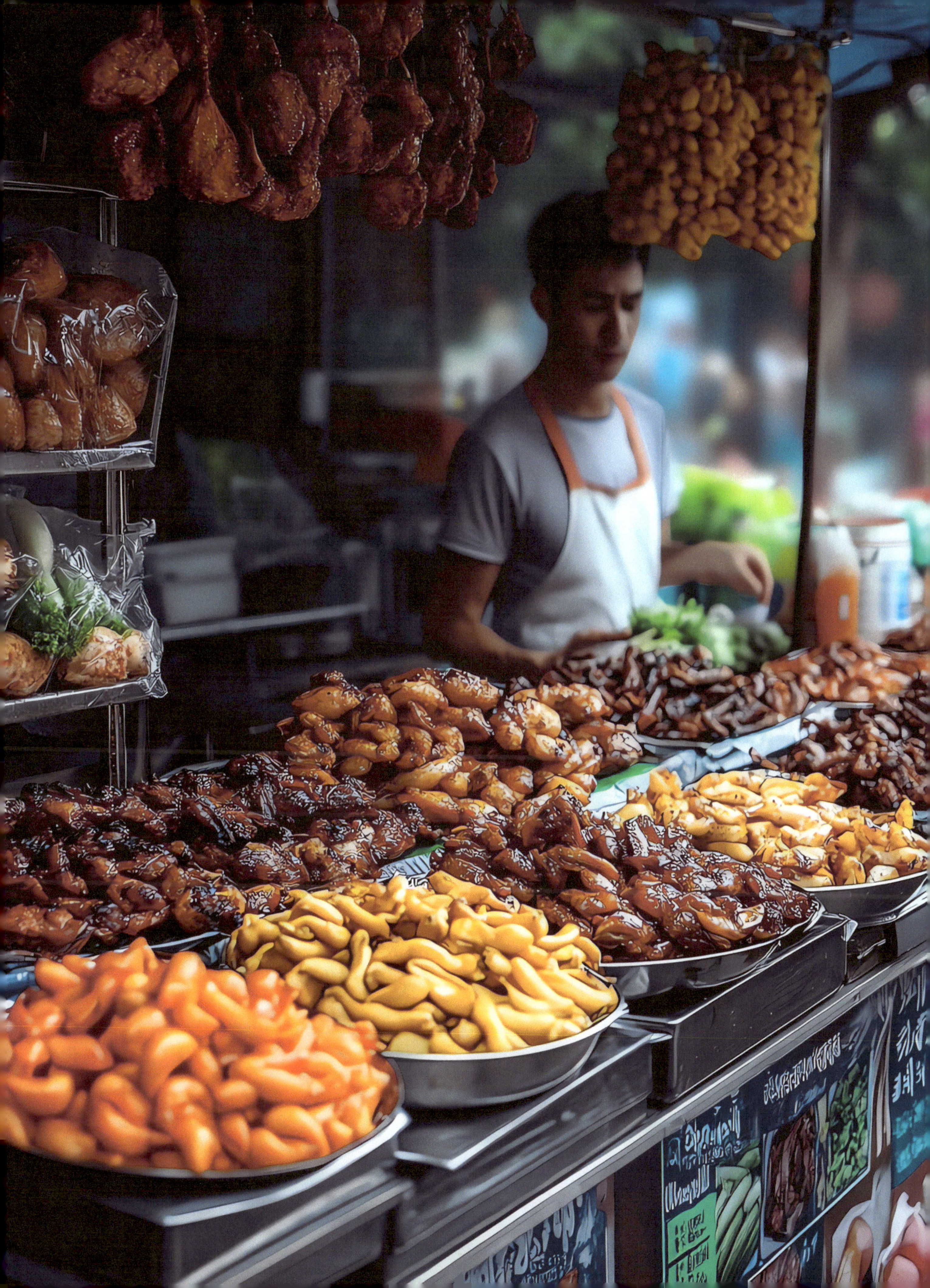

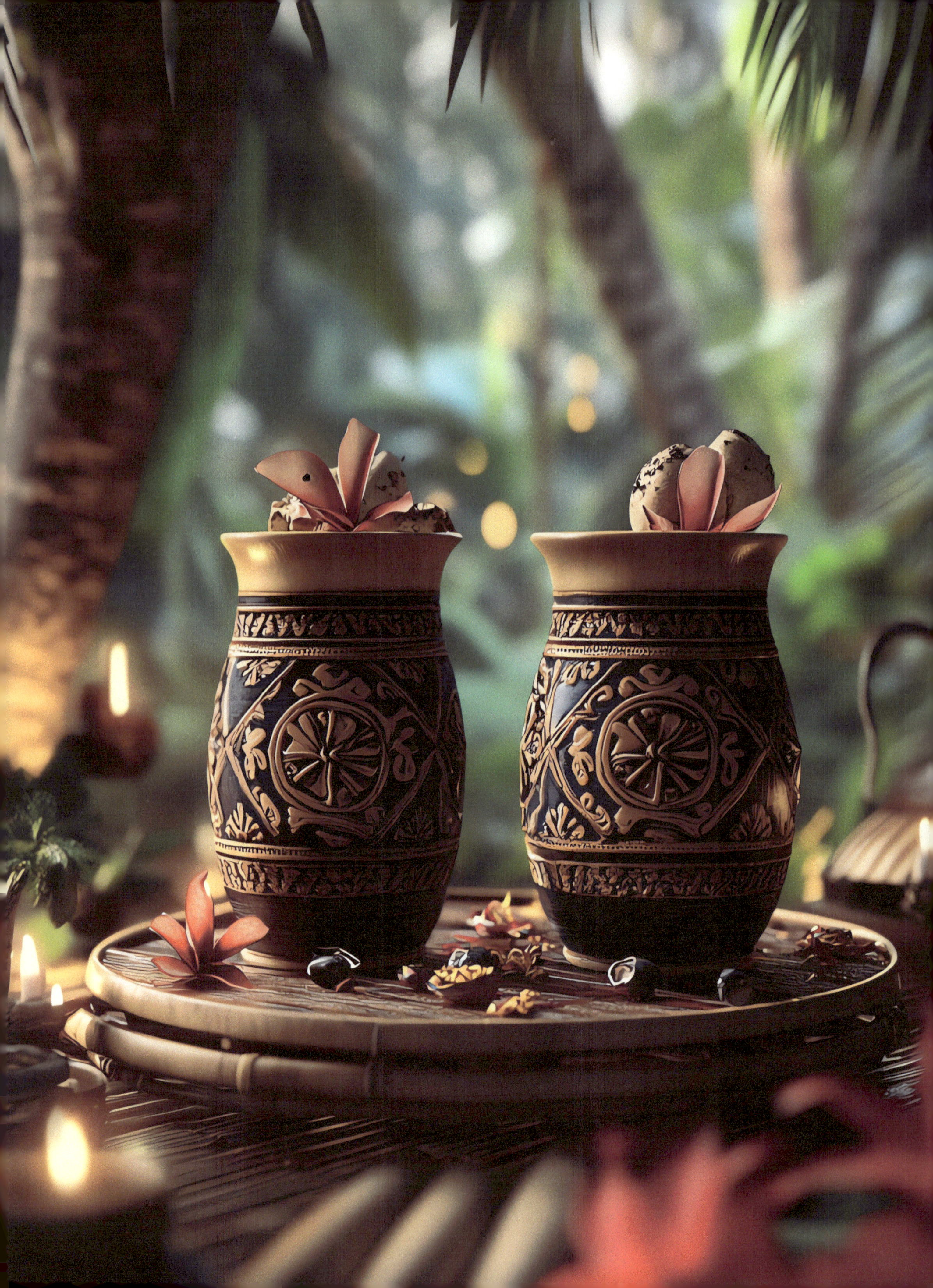

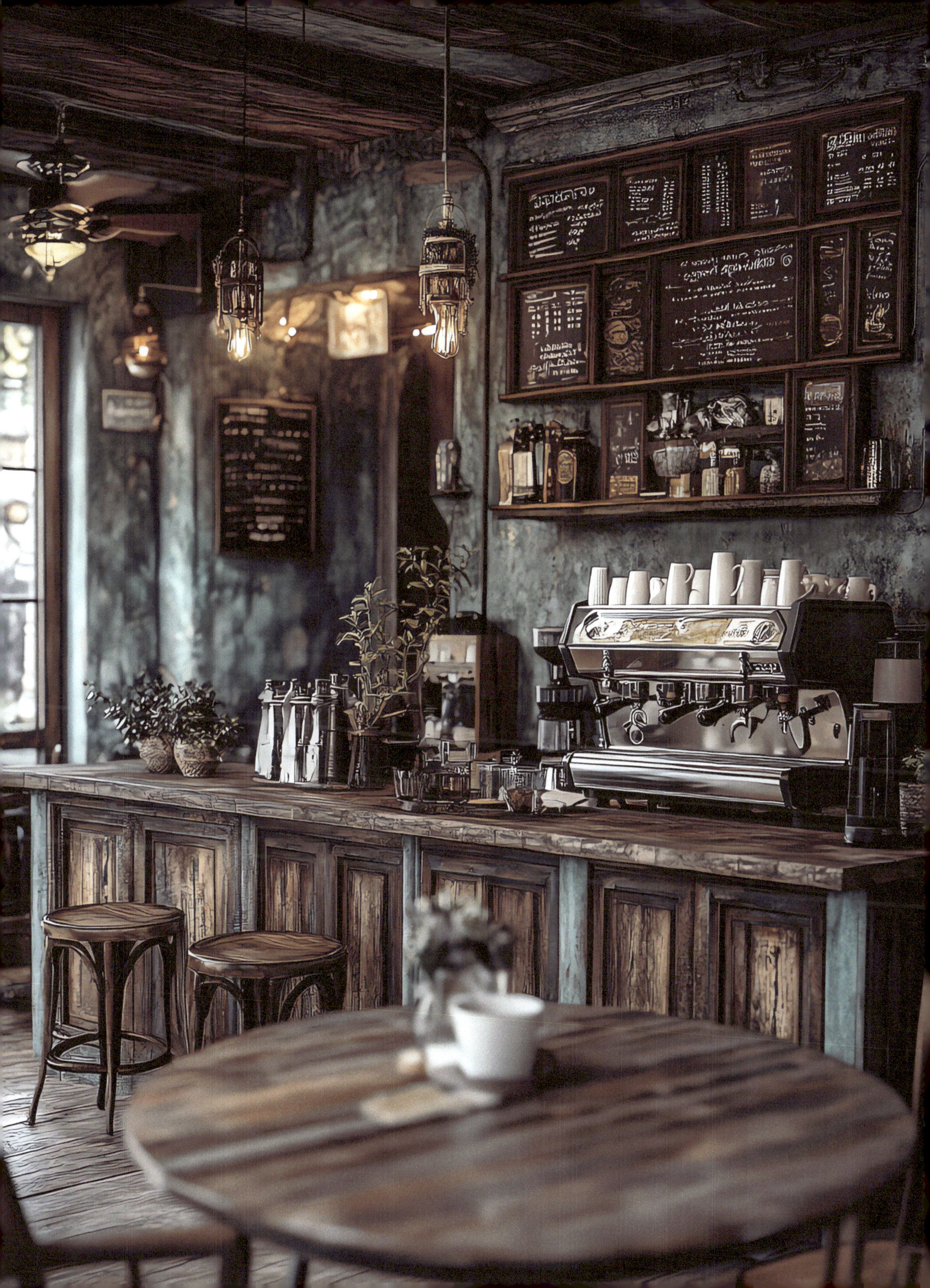

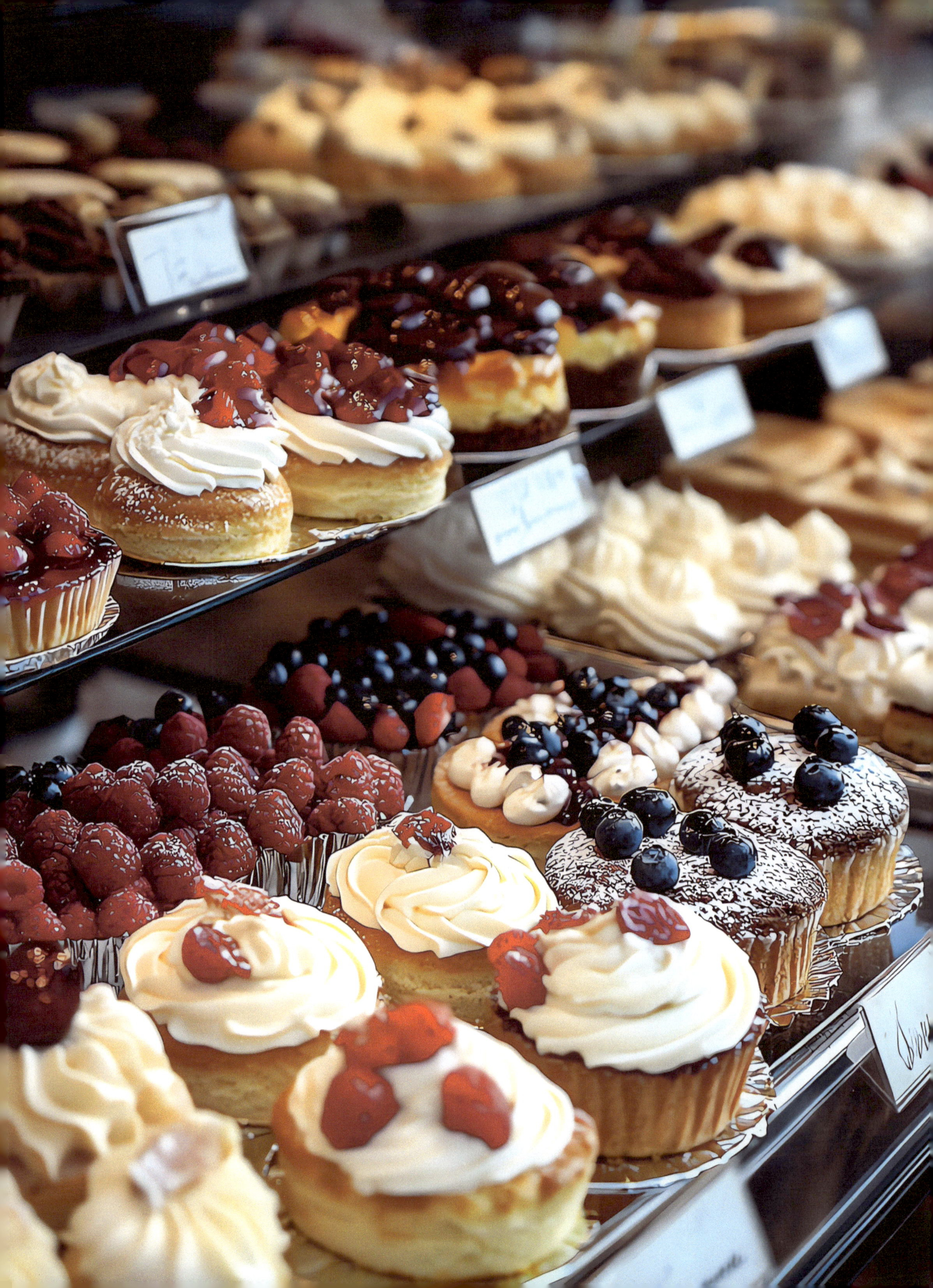

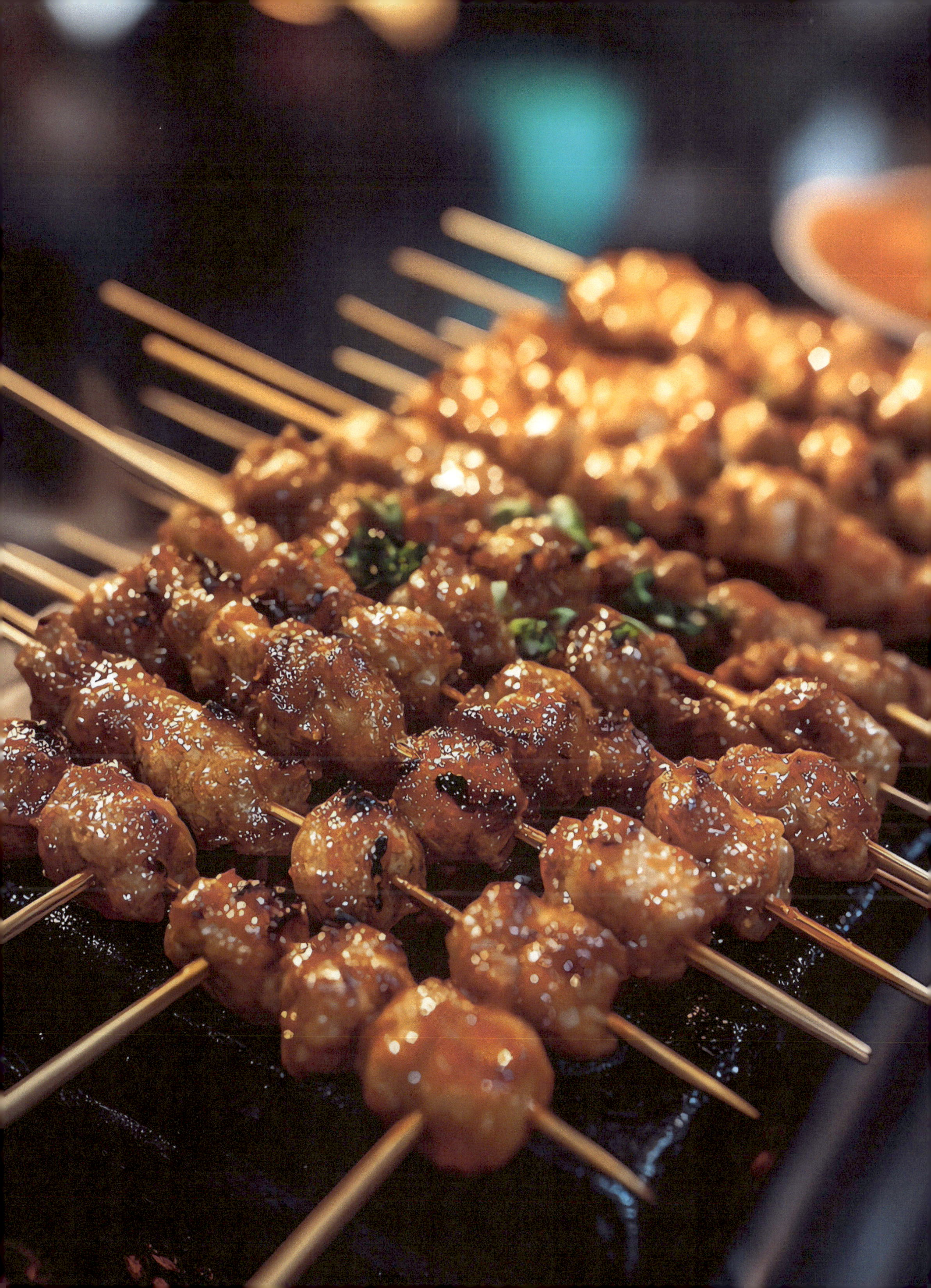

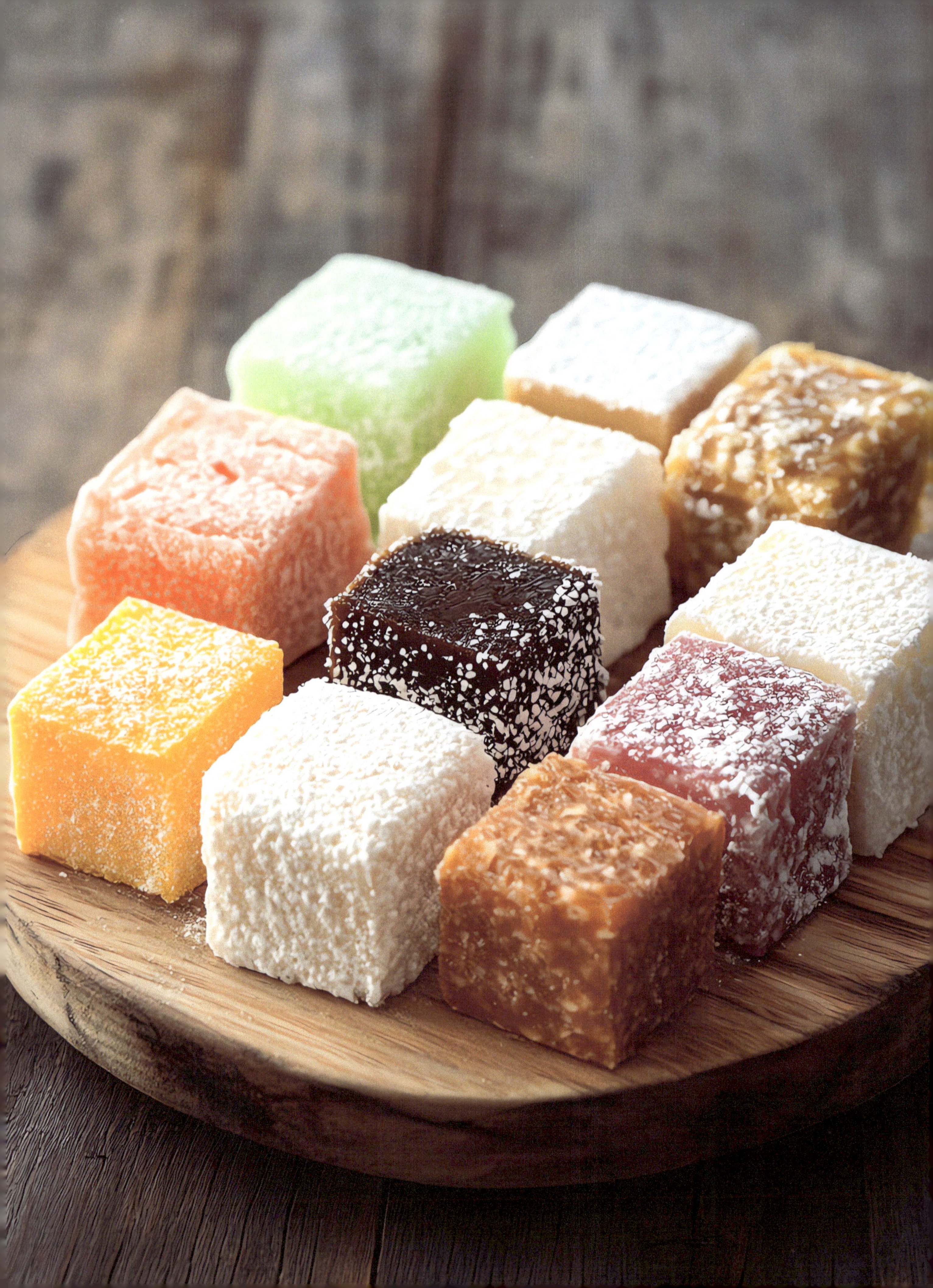

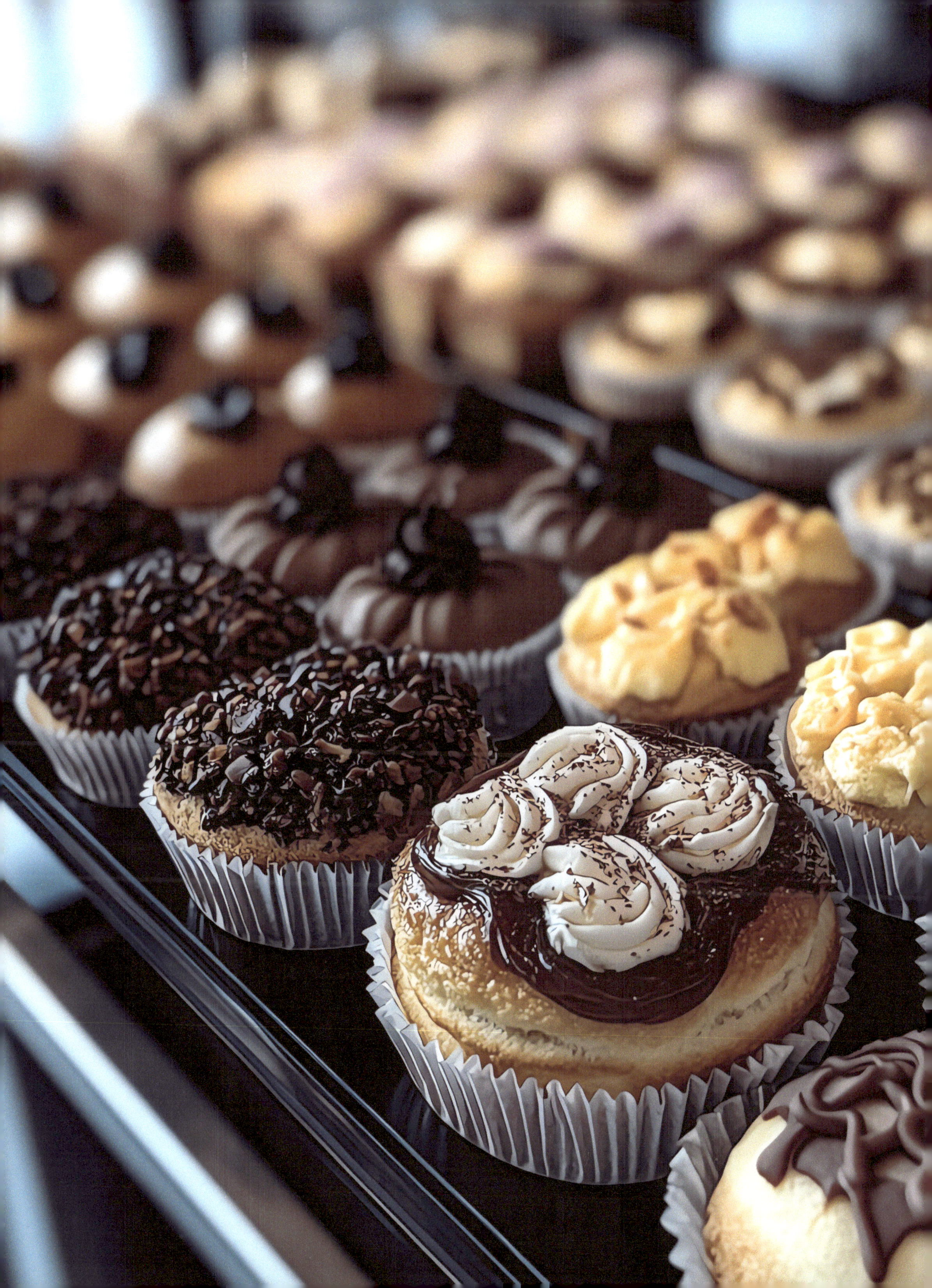

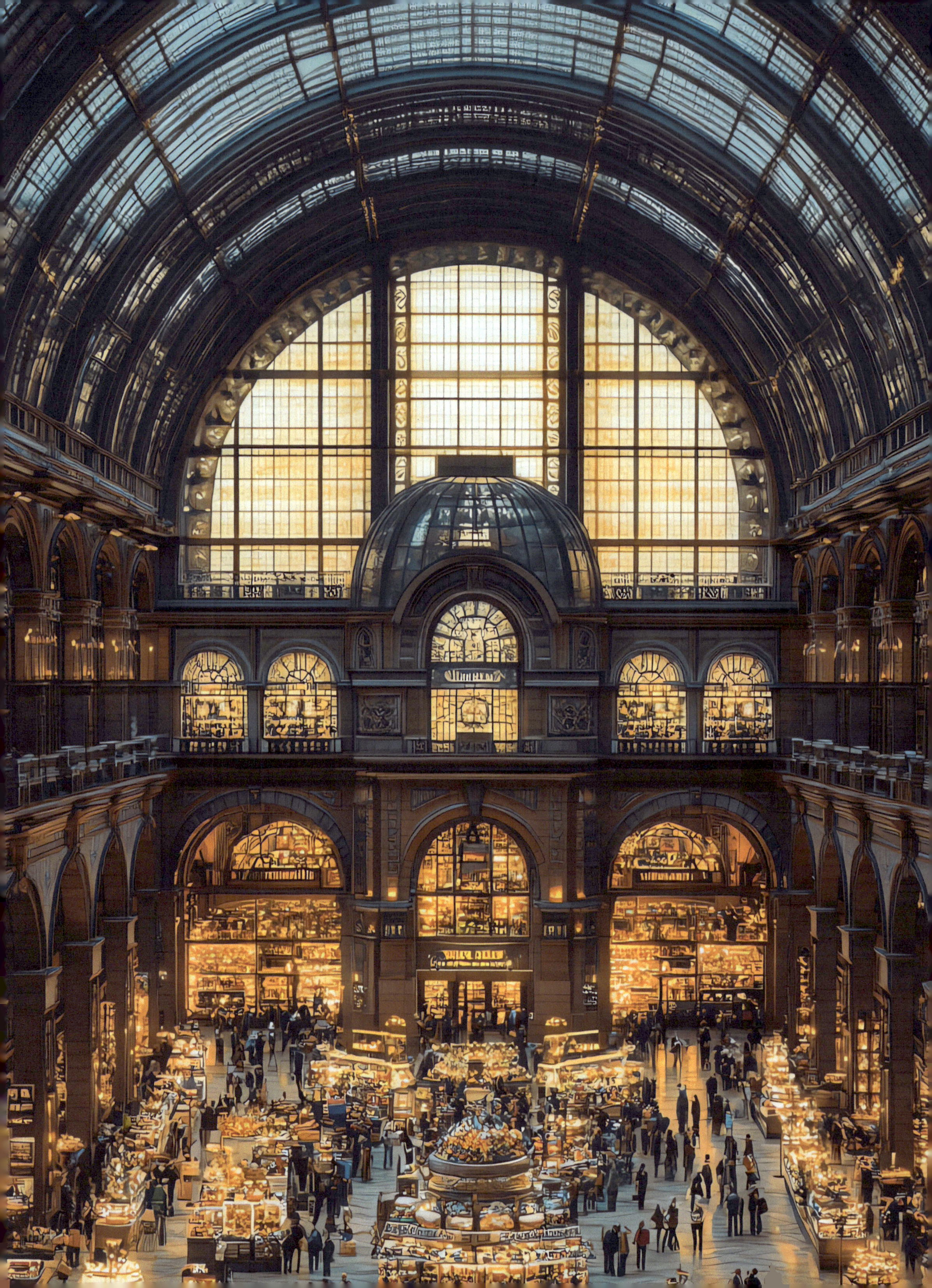

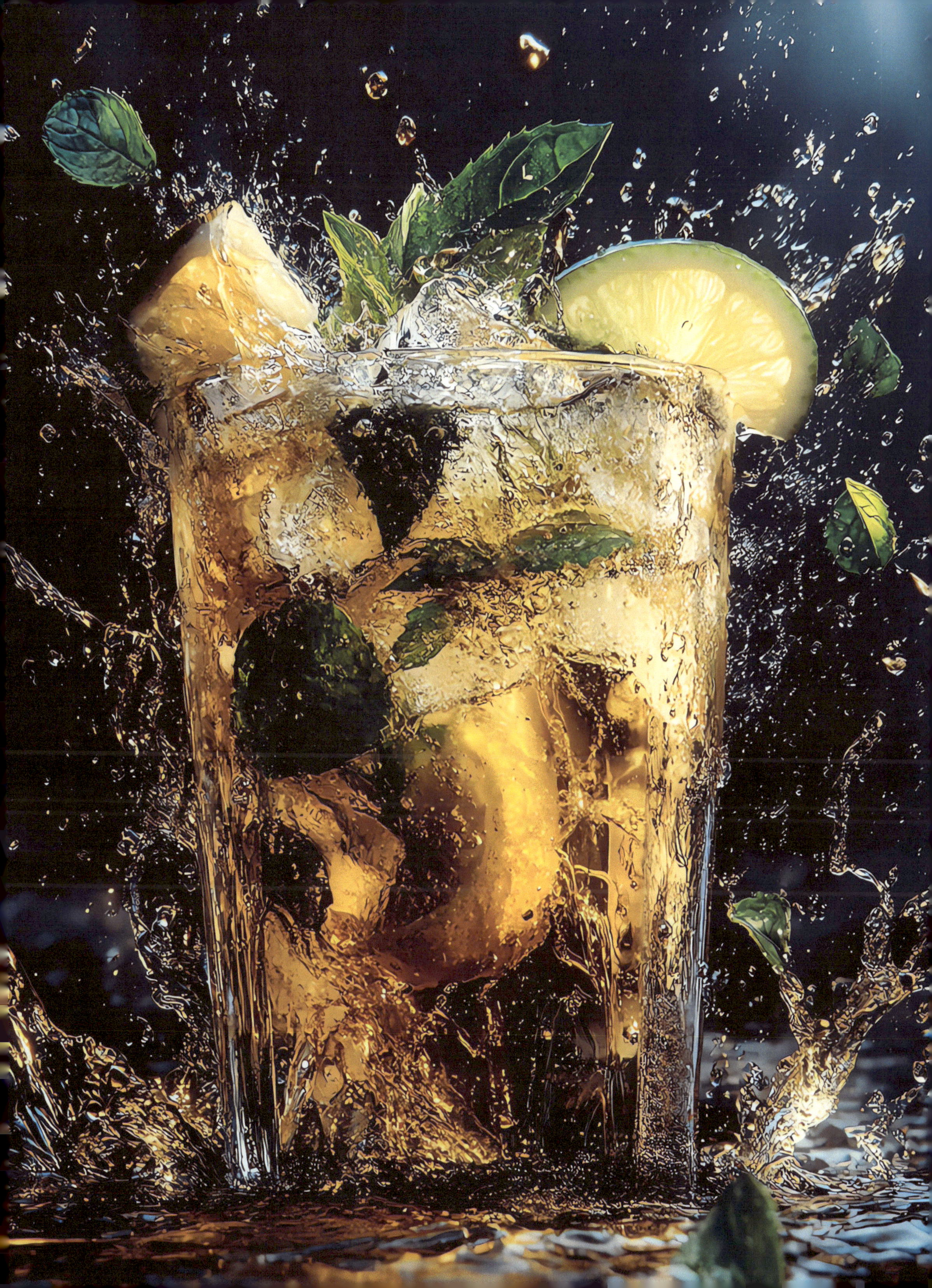

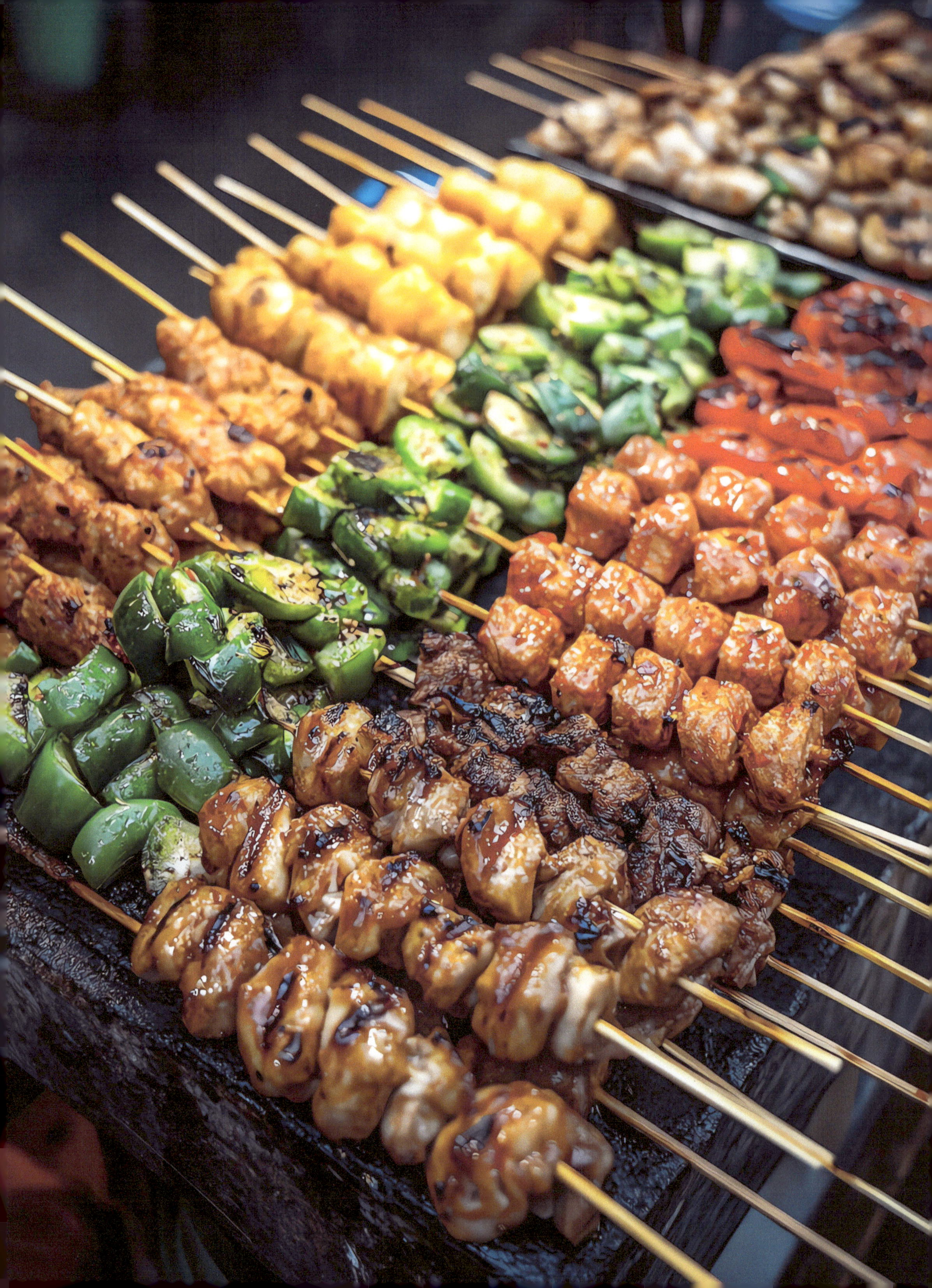

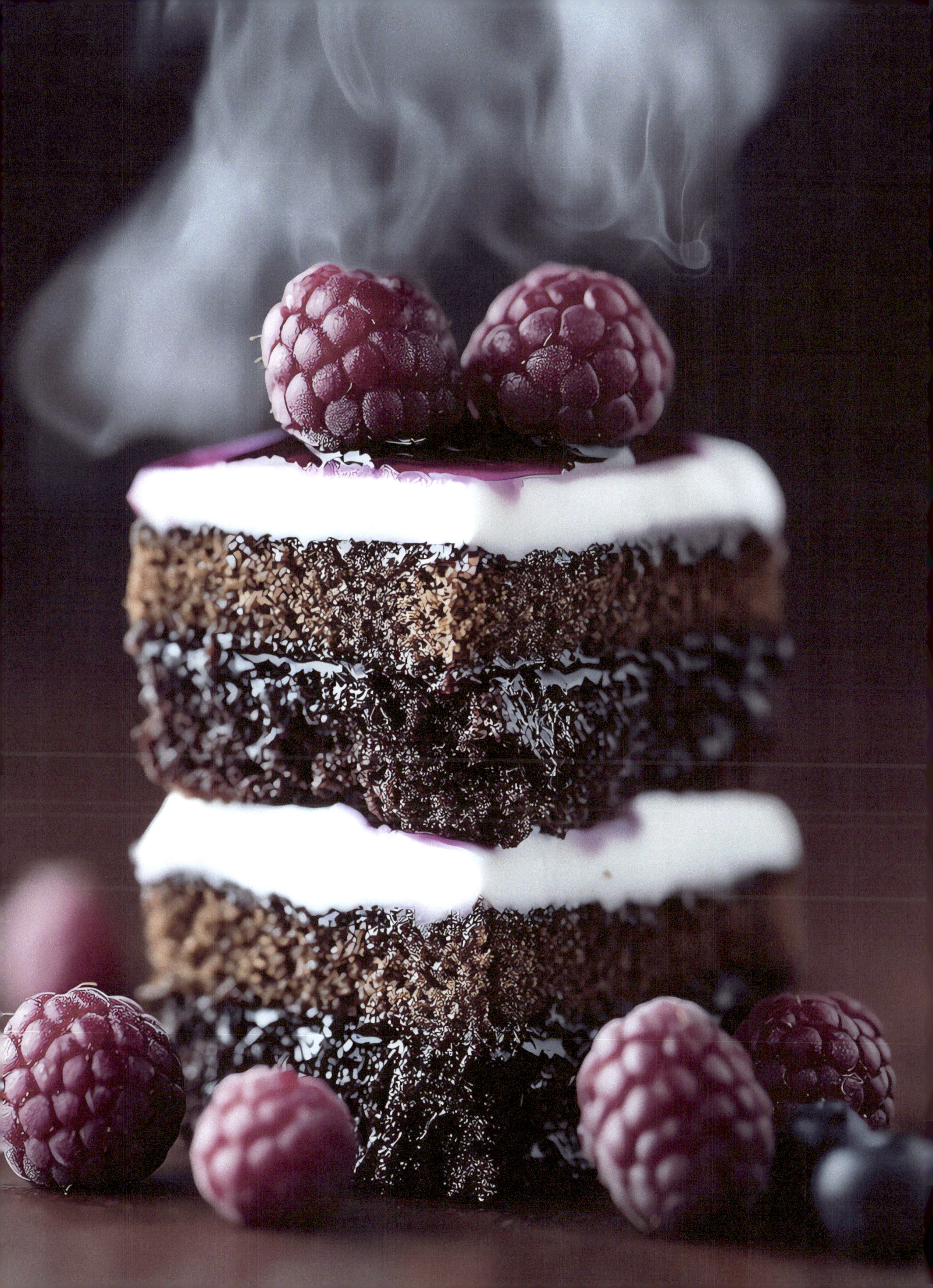

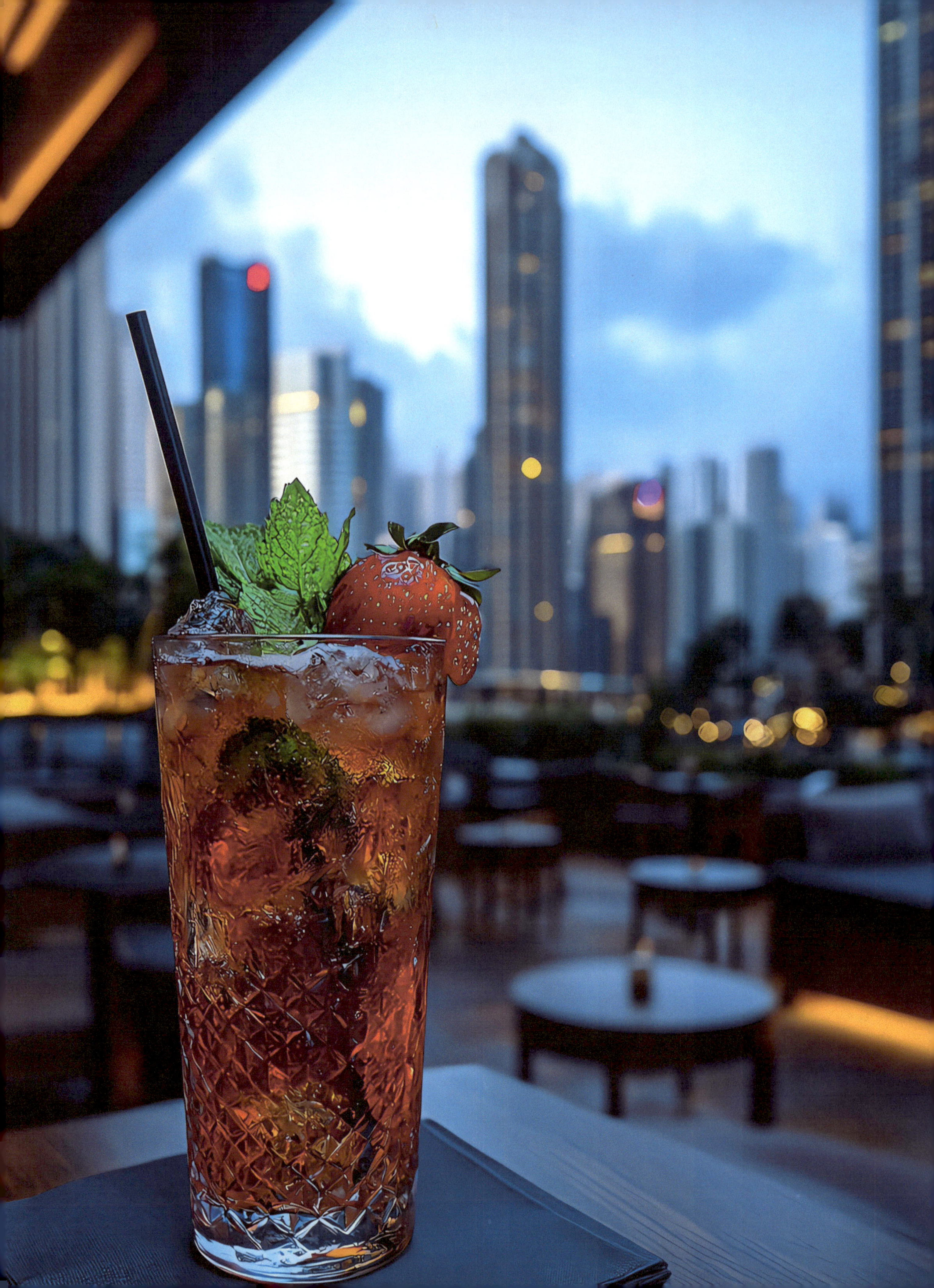

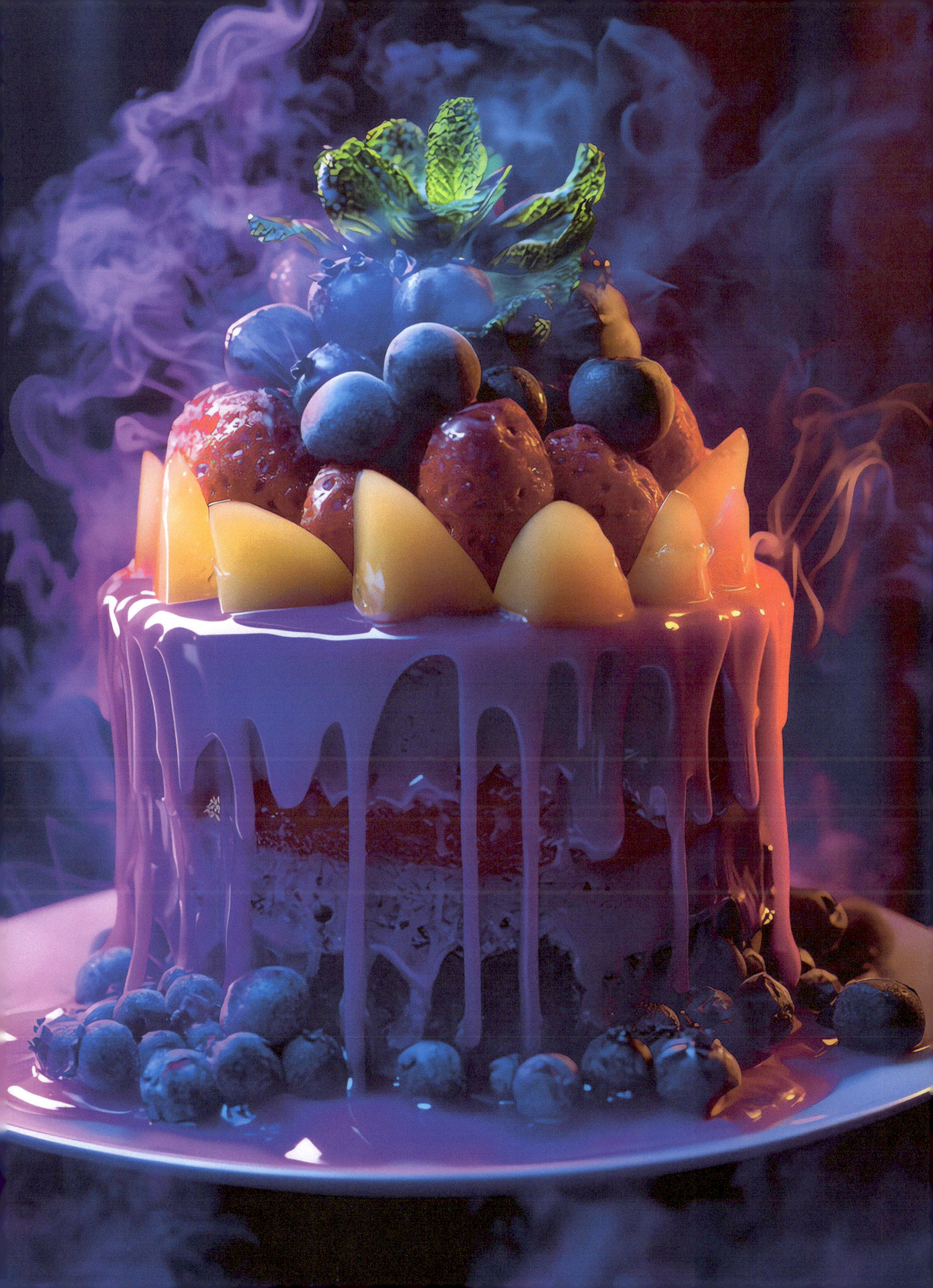

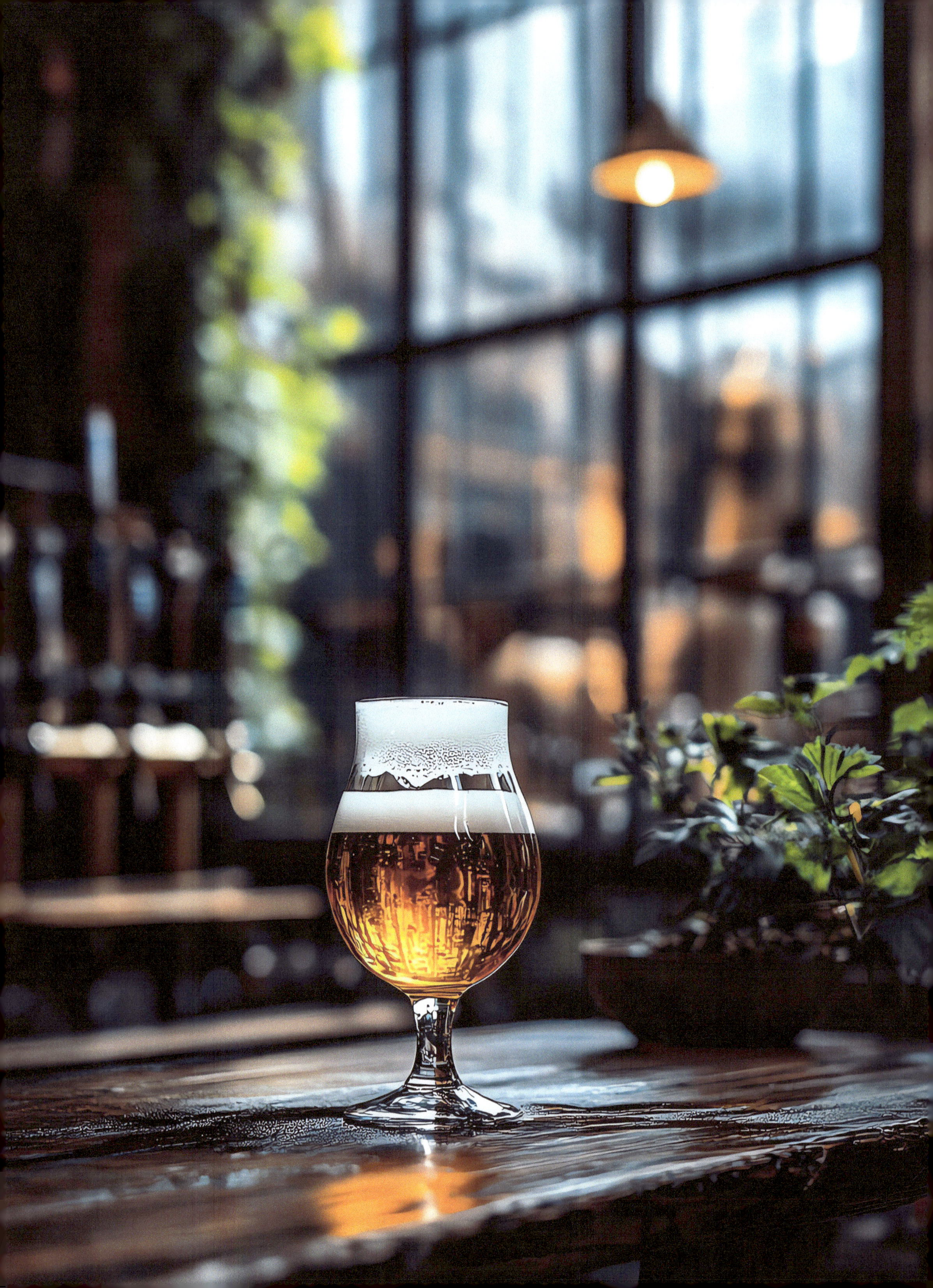

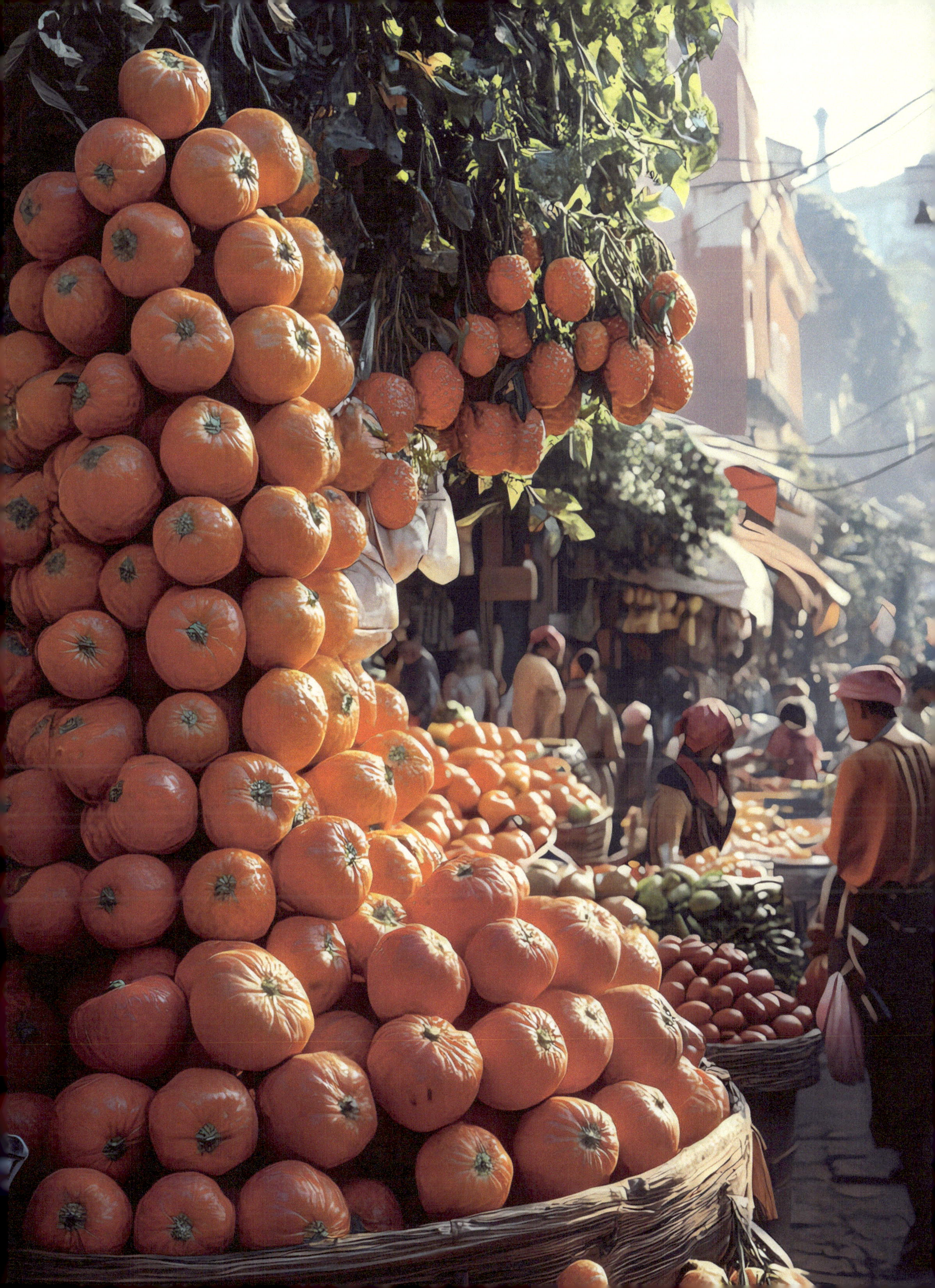

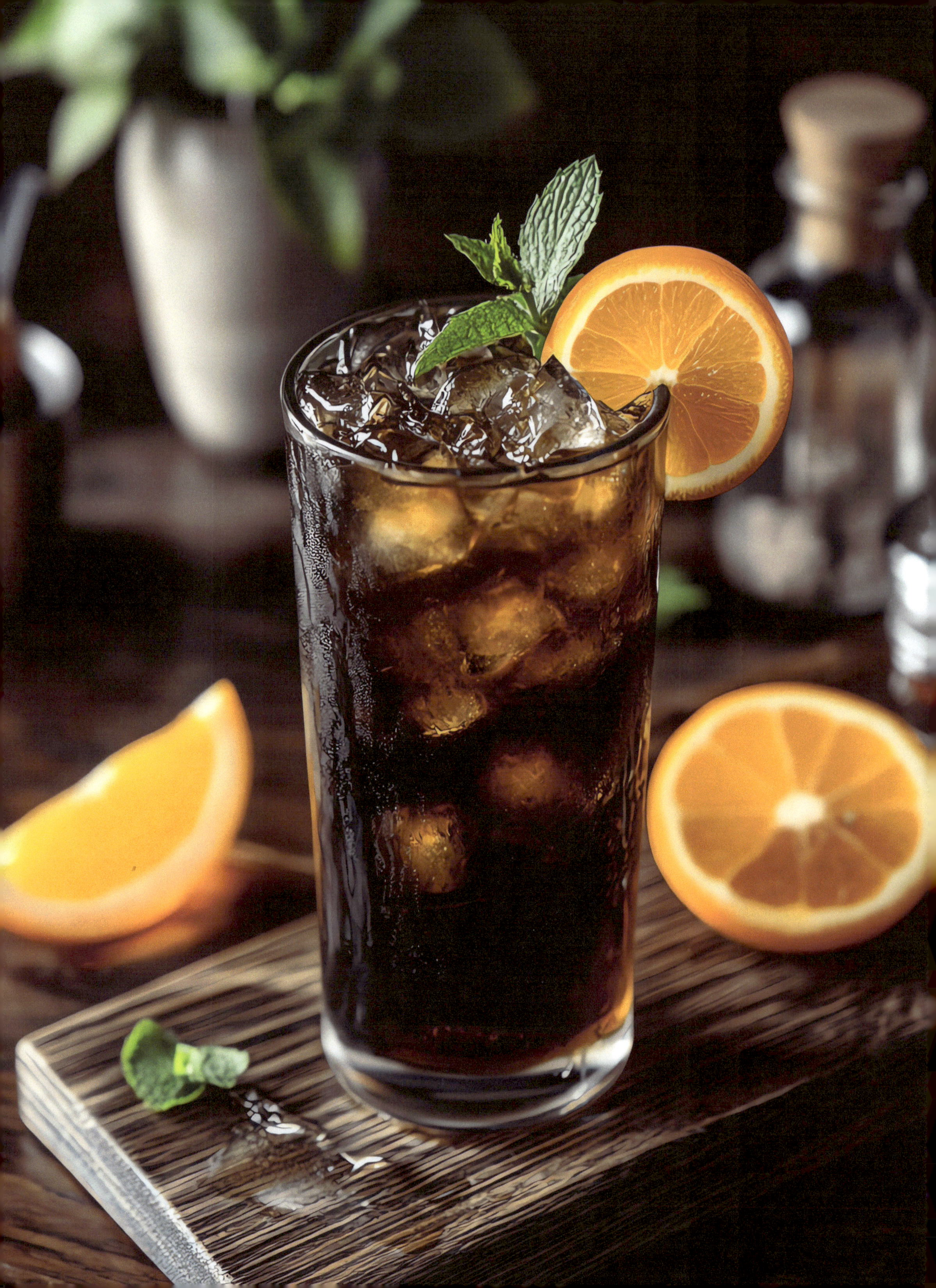